WHAT PEOPLE ARE SAYING ABOUT
Selling to the C-Suite

"The business world is drowning in a flood of sales books. The trouble is that most of these books are about how to sell, without a clue about how customers buy, and so they do more harm than good. This book is different. It is firmly rooted in how people buy, and so it works. And an added bonus that particularly appeals to me: the book is based on research, which makes it rare and welcome."

—Neil Rackham, author of *SPIN Selling*
and seminal thinker on sales effectiveness

"As an educator on the college level teaching professional selling, I found this book to be invaluable if you are interested in learning how to sell to the top executives. Not only does it help you understand when to engage the executive, it also tells you how to get access. If that was not enough, the book also focuses on how to create value and build credibility with the executives. It is a must read for anyone who interacts with top executives."

—Dan C. Weilbaker, PhD, Professor Emeritus of Sales,
Northern Illinois University

"This book is like a one-day MBA in Selling to Executives. A must read for sales professionals—both new and experienced—who want to get better at their craft."

—Tom Martin, President, Strategy 2 Revenue, and former
President of North America, Miller Heiman, Inc.

"Sales professionals who align with key executive decision makers early in the sales process have a higher win rate and make more money than their peers. Steve and Nic have meticulously researched and distilled the best practices that distinguish the salespeople who can sell at the executive level and are seen as Trusted Advisors. Credibility is the foundation of being a Trusted Advisor. *Selling to the C-Suite* lays out when and how to access executives, as well as how to establish credibility and value."

—Bill Walden, Worldwide Sales Operations, HP Software

"If Sun Tzu lived today, he would write this book. Chinese executives seek relationships to help their personal agenda and reduce their risk. *Selling to the C-Suite* is full of sage advice from two master practitioners on how to become a 'relationship master,' but most importantly, it is based on the executive's view. We were honored to partner in China on the research project, and this book brings those secrets to life in exciting ways."

—Anne An 安欣, Director Marketing,
Tsinghua SEM, and former manager of the
Hewlett-Packard Business School, Beijing, China

"A straightforward, pragmatic approach on how to gain and retain access to the executive level. Those new to executive sales will find a game plan they can use immediately. Veterans who regularly call on executives will use this book to sharpen their game."

—Chip Brubaker, Global Head of Sales
Enablement Delivery, Ericsson

"Too many salespeople have no idea if they're winning or losing, and it's usually because they're meeting the wrong people and asking the wrong questions too low down the food chain. As a result, their sales forecasts are no better than a lottery. This book pulls no punches in showing why sales and marketing fails to connect to executives, and what to do about it."

—Gordon Clubb, Managing Director, Genesys Australia & New Zealand

"I finished this book in one sitting; it is easy to read, and I was very impressed. It holds practical advice on how to get to the decision makers in the context of sales, but also applies in many other situations where the objective is influence. Having learned these lessons the hard way while transforming a Chinese state-owned enterprise into a globally competitive business, I wish this book had been available when I first started!"

—Geoff Watson, former General Manager,
Alcoa Bohai Aluminum Industries, China

"Nic Read and Dr. Bistritz show us how to reach out to executives using ideas from those executives. It's proven, and it works."

—Andy Sim, Head of Networking Business, Asia Pacific Japan, Dell EMC

"We hear a lot about being a Trusted Advisor, but what does that really mean? The authors clearly define that role with the insight, definition, and actions required to establish and sustain credible value-based engagements with senior executives. If your success depends on being engaged early in your customer's decision process and you're in a market that demands value-based differentiation, then this is a must read."

—Gary Summy, President, Move the Needle, LLC
and Former Director of the Strategic
Account Management Association (SAMA)

"Nothing on your shelf right now will tell you more about why salespeople fail to engage with CXOs, or what they need to do to earn the role of Trusted Advisor. Supported by revealing research and cutting insights, Read and Bistritz take you on a journey to discover why salespeople fail to engage with CXOs, and provide practical advice on what they need to do to earn their way in."

—Hugh Macfarlane, author of *The Leaky Funnel*
and Founder & CEO of Align.me

"This book offers something for every salesperson no matter how long they've been selling. For the new entrant to the profession, it offers proven tips for getting to the executive suite. For the seasoned salesperson, it provides time-honored techniques for staying there!"

—Karen Jackson, former Director of Business Development,
Americas, Computer Sciences Corporation (CSC)

"To not adopt these concepts puts you at risk of being left out in the lobby, while your competitor is in the client's boardroom."

—Michael Boland, coauthor of *Get-Real Selling*

"Finally, a book on selling to executives that isn't built on yesterday's traditional sales thinking! Anyone who's serious about the business of selling—as it exists today—needs to read this book."

—Jerry Stapleton, President, Stapleton Resources,
and author of *From Vendor to Business Resource*

"This book clearly explains the nature of different relationships within an organization and is a great guide to navigating your way through them to increase your prospect of making a sale. In my experience, the depth and breadth of your relationship as a Trusted Advisor best ensures your selling success. I also particularly liked the comment that marketing executives need to understand that marketing should be about making money."

—Alan Isaac, Chairman, KPMG New Zealand (retired)

"Most of what's out there from the experts on selling to executives is as dated as the cassette tapes we heard their message on the first time! *Selling to the C-Suite* offers a fresh, Internet-age view on why selling at the top matters so much in today's global B2B sales environment. The authors shed new light on the realities that make selling to executives harder to do today than ever before, and offer street-level coaching on how to secure ongoing executive access to drive unrivaled leverage!"

—Tim Caito, Managing Director, Customer Strategy
and Success, Force Management

"This book is absolutely *on the button* in terms of relevance to any sales organization, as it dispels so many myths and reinvigorates a sales team's attention to the real art of selling. Sales staff at all levels should keep this by their bed or on their desk, and refer to it daily!"

—Andrew Moon, Executive Director, Movers & Shakers Network

"The book puts into words what successful sales reps practice—mostly unaware of doing so. As a salesman and trainer, I love how it is able to generate a *that's it!* moment for both battle-hardened and new reps, especially summarized points that they can quickly act on."

—Ian Loh, Alliances Director, South Asia, Dell EMC

"If you've always wondered how the other sales guy got to the CEO and you didn't, start reading this book and earn serious commissions!"

—Lindsay Lyon, Managing Director,
Shark Shield, and former General Manager,
Commercial Sales, Hewlett-Packard Australia

"If ever there were insights into the minds of today's executives, this book is it. Based on solid research, Steve Bistritz and Nic Read share with you what today's executives are thinking, how to get in front of them, and what to do when you get there. The appendixes alone should be a mandatory read for any high-level sales representative."

—Gary Connor, author of *Sales: Games and Activities for Trainers*

"How quickly we fall into a comfort zone of selling features and benefits, but in most cases this just won't cut it at the executive level. In a world where the marketing and sales functions are being reshaped by the impact of the Internet, this book provides timely guidance, backed up by research into what drives decision makers at the top. After reading this book, you will find yourself taking lessons from it straight to your next prospect meeting—and it works!"

—Bill McNamara, CEO, Marketing Decisions, Eloqua distributor

"This is a very practical approach to calling on executives. The authors tell us why it is important and how to do it. Getting access to the executive level is one battle, but knowing what to talk to them about when you get there is another. This book provides a road map. Every organization calling on Fortune 1000 companies needs this information."

—Renie McClay, Adjunct Professor at Roosevelt University and
Concordia University, and former president of the Professional
Society for Sales and Marketing Training (SMT)

"In today's selling environment, having the confidence and the knowledge to sell at the C-level is often the difference between success and failure for B2B sales teams. In a clear, concise, and compelling way, Steve Bistritz and Nic Read solve the mysteries surrounding selling to senior executives and provide all the tools and resources needed to access, leverage, and create winning relationships in the corner office. Definitely a must read."

—Chris Deren, CEO, Clarity Learning Systems

"Great information on a critical topic for all salespeople. The sale to an executive is made during the questioning process, not in your product presentation. You can't sell anything to an executive until you have first sold yourself."

—Duane Sparks, author of *Action Selling*
and Chairman, The Sales Board

"More and more sales organizations are realizing that the most effective means to *get ink* is to start at the top of the management chain and work your way down to exactly the right office. The trouble is, many sales professionals are skittish about making contact with anyone in a position greater than middle management for fear of being rejected. *Selling to the C-Suite* is a no-nonsense road map for sales pros who are ready to try something highly effective. Steve and Nic have put together a powerful guide that will soon have you aiming for the executive suite with confidence."

—Dan Walker, President, The MarComm Store

"The data is real, the suggestions are right on target, and the tools are designed to help any sales professional succeed in selling to the CXO level. Identifying the relevant executive and becoming a trusted business advisor take dedication and determination. This book has outlined all the necessary steps to guide you for several years to come. I'm buying a copy for each member of my sales organization, and I'd recommend this book to anyone who wants to be the best in their field."

—Vince Melograna, VP Business Development,
The Revenue Accelerator

"Bistritz and Read are world-class experts in the discipline of selling to executives. Savvy sales professionals, as well as the senior executives they report to, will value *Selling to the C-Suite* as *the* guide to gaining and maintaining access to those most-influential members of the customer's executive team—the inner circle."

—David Stein, former CEO and Founder,
ES Research Group, Inc.

"In the current changing market, we all need to show our unique value to customers. To help them become true Trusted Advisors, all of our salespeople will learn from this book."

—Atsuhiro Ozeki, former General Manager,
Fuji Xerox Learning Institute Inc., Tokyo, Japan

"Very insightful and practical. I can see this book being invaluable to all sales professionals, especially those who focus on the B2B arena. Plus it's written in plain English with good examples that help explain the intricacies, theories, and art of selling."

—Kevin Fong, former CEO,
China Automobile Association,
a subsidiary of IAG

"Nic Read and Dr. Bistritz have done a masterful job summarizing how to approach and sell to executives. If you read this and apply its secrets, you'll win more, more of the time."

—Michael Gallagher, President,
The Stevie Awards for Sales & Customer Service

"*Selling to the C-Suite* is the ultimate resource for those who want to get through to the most powerful decision makers in today's business world. Globalization is happening now, and Nic Read and Dr. Bistritz have the experience, the know-how, and the research to guide you."

—Dan Hill, President, Sensory Logic, Inc., and author
of *Emotionomics: Winning Hearts and Minds*

"Based on real research and great insights into how and why executives buy, Steve and Nic provide a pathway to success for anyone selling at the executive level. It doesn't matter where you are in your sales career, you will benefit from this book."

—Paul Aldo, PhD, President, Executive Presence

"Steve and Nic provide a great history lesson that helps us understand why marketing and sales is different in the new millennium and provides the research background to prove their points. If you want to become effective at the C-Suite, this book and its references, models, and tools are incredible."

—Jim Graham, former Chief Learning Officer, R.R. Donnelley

SELLING

TO THE

C-SUITE

WHAT EVERY EXECUTIVE
WANTS YOU TO KNOW
ABOUT SUCCESSFULLY
SELLING TO THE TOP

SECOND EDITION

NICHOLAS A.C. READ
STEPHEN J. BISTRITZ, EdD

New York Chicago San Francisco Athens London Madrid
Mexico City Milan New Delhi Singapore Sydney Toronto

1 2 3 4 5 6 7 8 9   LCR   23 22 21 20 19 18

ISBN   978-1-260-11642-7
MHID   1-260-11642-5

e-ISBN   978-1-260-11640-3
e-MHID   1-260-11640-9

McGraw-Hill books are available at special quantity discounts to use as premiums and sales promotions, or for use in corporate training programs. To contact a representative, please visit the Contact Us pages at www.mhprofessional.com.

Library of Congress Cataloging-in-Publication Data

Names: Read, Nicholas A. C., author. | Bistritz, Stephen J., author.
Title: Selling to the C-Suite : what every executive wants you to know about
    successfully selling to the top / Nicholas Read and Stephen Bistritz.
Description: Second edition. | New York : McGraw-Hill, [2018] | Includes
    bibliographical references and index.
Identifiers: LCCN 2017051245| ISBN 9781260116427 (alk. paper) | ISBN
    1260116425
Subjects: LCSH: Selling. | Sales executives.
Classification: LCC HF5438.25 .R38 2018 | DDC 658.85--dc23 LC record available
    at https://lccn.loc.gov/2017051245

For two Richards.
One filled the sails with winds of possibility.
The other steadied the helm.
—NR

To my dear wife, Claire,
with thanks, gratitude, and love
for 50 wonderful years of marriage!
—SB

Contents

FOREWORD TO THE FIRST EDITION   vii

PREFACE   xi

ACKNOWLEDGMENTS   xix

CHAPTER 1

WHEN DO EXECUTIVES GET INVOLVED
IN THE DECISION PROCESS?   1

CHAPTER 2

MARKETING TO THE C-SUITE   27

CHAPTER 3

UNDERSTANDING WHAT
EXECUTIVES WANT   53

CHAPTER 4

HOW TO FIND THE RELEVANT
EXECUTIVE   77

CONTENTS

CHAPTER 5

HOW TO GAIN ACCESS TO
THE C-SUITE   99

CHAPTER 6

HOW TO ESTABLISH CREDIBILITY
WITH THE C-SUITE   119

CHAPTER 7

HOW TO CREATE VALUE
FOR THE C-SUITE   143

CHAPTER 8

CULTIVATING LOYALTY AT
THE C-SUITE   171

AFTERWORD   191

APPENDIX A
GUIDE TO CLIENT DISCOVERY   199

APPENDIX B
TOOLS FOR BUILDING THE EXECUTIVE RELATIONSHIP   215

RECOMMENDED READING   241
RECOMMENDED ASSOCIATIONS AND ORGANIZATIONS   247
NOTES   251
INDEX   255

Foreword to the First Edition

Neil Rackham

Sales has grown up a lot in the last 10 years, and this book is a good example of just how far selling has come. When the manuscript first landed on my desk, I looked at the title, *Selling to the C-Suite,* and I couldn't suppress a groan. "Another collection of impractical advice about how to get in front of any key executive without even trying," I thought. And you can't blame me for being skeptical. Almost without exception, books on how to get access to "The Man," "VITO," "the fox," or a dozen other names for the top dog whose signature can change your life, have been mediocre and unrealistic. So, I must admit, I started reading with very low expectations.

By the time I reached the end of the first chapter, all that had changed. Three things were immediately evident:

- There is a refreshing realism about the authors' advice. No gimmicks, no tricks, no smoke and mirrors. Selling successfully at C-level is hard, thoughtful, and strategic, and the book offers none of the usual unrealistic silver bullets.

- The ideas are based on research, not on anecdotes. The authors interviewed hundreds of senior executives to learn about their buying practices, and, for this alone, the book is worth its weight in commission checks.
- It is one of the few books that actually demonstrates an understanding of selling in a global business environment. There are cases and examples from—among other places—China, Europe, and Australia. Everybody says we must think globally. Nic Read and Stephen Bistritz have been doing it. They have been working all over the world, and they really understand global business because they live it every day.

Selling to the C-Suite comes at the right moment. Nic Read and Stephen Bistritz have been developing this material for 10 years, and they couldn't have timed their publication better. There are three intersecting factors that put the book at the center of a perfect storm that is changing selling in fundamental ways.

THE ECONOMY IN CRISIS

These are unprecedented times when even the superconfident economic gurus readily confess that they don't know what's going on or how long it will be before that comforting word "normal" can be safely used again. Prediction is rapidly going out of style. Yet I'll venture one confident prediction based on the history of every economic downturn for the past century. When the economy goes down, the decisions go up. A purchasing decision that is made in good times at a middle management level requires active participation from the top when company survival is at stake. Selling cycles take longer, and customers become risk averse. In this environment, the ability to sell effectively at C-level has never been so important. The advice in this book can make all the difference. Here's just one example. From their research, Read and Bistritz identify where in the sales cycle C-level executives get involved, why they get involved, and what this means for an effective sales strategy. Very few of the salespeople I work with understand the dynamics of top management involvement, and this book will certainly help them.

THE NEW CEO ROLE

In the good old days, CEOs could succeed by looking for improvement inside the company. By cutting away fat and by introducing systems, processes, TQM, and the like, their organizations became lean, mean, and competitive. Today, with a few endangered exceptions in the much vilified financial and pharmaceutical industries, the fat is gone, and the company runs like clockwork. So how does a CEO make an impact? The fashionable answer has been acquisition. Grow the company by buying your competition. But, in today's environment, raising the capital for acquisition has become next to impossible. What's more, the track record of acquisitions has proved spotty and questionable. With the traditional growth strategies unavailable or discredited, CEOs are now turning outward. The new role of the CEO is to create value at the organization's boundaries, to radically change relationships with suppliers, customers, and alliance partners. This creates significant opportunities for the few salespeople who can relate at an enterprise level with their customers. The authors worked closely with Hewlett-Packard and saw, firsthand, how the top hundred HP accounts brought in upwards of $13 billion in 2005. To generate this kind of revenue, the account executives for each of these accounts not only had to work at the C-level in order to understand the customers' strategies and politics, but they also had to use extraordinary creativity to help their customers find new value from their collaboration. I detect much of their experience in the pages of *Selling to the C-Suite*.

THE VALUE CREATION IMPERATIVE

The final factor that makes this such a timely book is a trend that has been gathering pace for several years. The old role of sales—to show customers why your products and services are better than those of your competitors—is no longer viable. It's too expensive, and customers don't want it. Salespeople who still cling to this traditional role (I call them "talking brochures," while the authors here use the curiously similar term "walking brochures"—take your pick) are failing everywhere. In their place, the new salespeople are highly skilled value creators, who live by ingeniously solving customer problems. The measure of these new salespeople is the value they create and, to create maximum value, they must understand the issues and concerns of their C-Suite customers. This book is timely and essential reading for them.

Neil Rackham
Author of *SPIN Selling*
Visiting Professor of Sales and Marketing,
Portsmouth Business School
Visiting Professor of Sales Strategy, Cranfield University

Preface

If you've ever tried and failed to meet a senior executive that you needed to sell to, this book is for you. If you've managed to nail a first meeting at the C-level, but the executive later froze you out, you'll learn what went wrong and how to solve it. And even if you've already mastered the executive call, don't relax just yet; the rise of globalized, nontraditional hierarchies and borderless organizations means that you may have mastered a set of skills for a world that no longer exists!

You owe it to yourself, to your employer, and, most important, to your clients to read, ponder, and apply the golden nuggets waiting to be discovered here. It's not the first book written on this topic, but it *is* the most relevant for today's global technology-enabled market, no matter whether you sell in Mumbai, Manchester, Melbourne, or Manhattan!

That's a pretty tall claim. Can we back it up? Like any salespeople worth their salt, we offer three solid validations:

1. *We've written this book from a combined 80 years of experience selling on corporate front lines around the world.* From IT, communications,

and professional services to banking, insurance, and manufacturing, between us we've carried a bag, beat the street, and
walked the talk for a variety of large-ticket business-to-business
solutions for more than five decades—and not just in one culture, but in many countries across Europe, the Middle East and
Africa, Asia–Pacific, North America, and Latin America. We have
enough war stories and frequent-flyer miles to know what we're
talking about.

2. *This book is based on empirical research.* We couldn't find any books
written on this topic that held anything more than personal
anecdotes of what the author did in her glory days. While trips
down Memory Lane may have some value, they tell you only the
salesperson's opinion about how executives buy. We wanted to dig
deeper and get inside the heads of living, breathing executives to
see what's really going on in there during the decision-making
process.

So we commissioned groundbreaking research of our own,
and jumped onto any other project team we could find where
executive buying habits were the focus of study, particularly
those run by Hewlett-Packard in North America; the Hewlett-
Packard Business School in Beijing, China; Target Marketing
Systems; the Kenan-Flagler School of Business at the University
of North Carolina; and the Center for Business & Industrial Marketing at Georgia State University.

After delving into the executive brain for 10 years, we're ready
to share with you what C-Suite leaders in 500 diverse companies
and government bodies told us (purchasing and middle managers were excluded) in response to interviews that asked probing
questions such as:

- *When do executives get involved in the buying process for major
  decisions?*
- *How do salespeople gain access to executives?*
- *How can salespeople establish credibility with executives?*

- *How can salespeople create value at the executive level?*
- *Is executive buying behavior consistent across cultures?*

As you do more of the things that senior executives respond to, you'll command greater credibility, close more business, and make more money.

3. *Thousands of sales professionals have already field-tested these concepts.* We decided that the best way to split-test our research was to turn the findings into two separate training workshops, market them independently, and compare the results of people applying them with real customers as a way of helping us isolate a distillation of best practices from disparate sources (information on these workshops can be found at www.sellxl.com and www .saleslabs.com). We discovered that it didn't matter what country, culture, industry, or economic situation the salesperson operated in. These principles work consistently.

We continue to receive e-mails from graduates about epic struggles that they fought and won against fierce competitors because they were able to get onto the executive's radar and raise the bar. We've selected two quick examples from opposite corners of the world to illustrate.

Karen, an account manager for a telecommunications carrier in Australia, told us:

> My major account was about to turn to a competitor. I'd tried everything to appease the client, but the contracts manager had found a better price from a smaller carrier, and in truth, as the big gorilla, we'd been arrogant in expecting that this client would never change suppliers. I was about to lose this large flagship account when I was sent to your training. I applied what I learned and was able to gain immediate access above the contracts manager to the senior executive who would be most affected by a change of supplier. Your process ran like

clockwork. I knew where I needed to steer the discussion and what to say, and this executive responded exactly as I hoped he would. The bottom line is that I saved the account, and I learned a valuable lesson about staying aligned with my customers. Several months later, the relationship is at an all-time high. I have no doubt that this is a direct result of what I learned from your research and your workshop.

Conny, a top account manager for a data warehousing vendor in Germany, shares this story:

I was selling to the IT managers in a major finance and insurance company. Their project had a budget of 200,000 Euro with a decision date 12 months away. After learning in your training how to become a business advisor to executives, I was able to rise above the operations level and find a middle-level sponsor who took me to the CEO. When I positioned my pitch around business outcomes instead of technology, my competitors were like ants at my feet. The CEO had wider issues than the IT manager knew about, more budget, and the ability to make the decision after just a few meetings. My sale expanded to 800,000 Euro, and I closed it within 6 months—higher and faster than I could ever have achieved without executive alignment.

Interesting isn't it? Salespeople like these were already experienced, they had sales managers whose job it was to coach them, and they'd already attended their company's sales induction and other training. And yet they still lacked the knowledge to excel with executives.

Why?

It's our observation that most traditional wisdom about selling to executives is actually at odds with what executives themselves tell us works. And that's a massive problem with the sales profession today. It's as if the last 50 years of corporate sales training has been based more on anecdotes and folklore than on any real science. So when we hear sales managers and trainers teach generalities like "always sell at the top," frankly, we cringe.

In a simpler time, when the guy running a business was the guy who owned the business (what we now call small and medium-sized enterprises, or SMEs), chances are that calling on the "very important top officer" would put you in the ballpark. But today's large companies can represent a labyrinth of global business units where politics, external advisors, and delegated authority affect the decision-making process in ways that were never considered by the collective wisdom of several decades ago.

Today, blindly calling on a senior executive *just because he's a senior executive* will do more harm than good. What if this executive has no skin in the game on this decision? What if it's a project that will never rise to his pay grade? What if he's already handed the project down to a competent subordinate and doesn't see the need to remain involved? What if he's too new in his role to have any political clout? What if he's about to retire and is merely a figurehead in the exit lounge or assigned to only the most insignificant special projects? What if he's recently made a few bad decisions, and any vendor he now sponsors will be tarred with the same brush?

It can cost you the deal if the guy at the top isn't the *relevant executive*. This relevant executive is the one who most feels the pain, most owns the problem you can solve, and will most richly reward you for providing a solution. The relevant executive will be someone with a combination of rank and political influence, with an internal network that allows her to initiate projects, kill projects, intervene in projects, and find funding, both in her own silo and across departmental boundaries. What the relevant executive wants, she gets. And the relevant executive isn't always found at the C-level. This is why "always sell at the top" can be your fastest ticket out of the race.

What's missing from the toolkits of today's road warriors is a set of simple approaches for identifying the relevant executive, enlisting the support of gatekeepers, getting past the roadblocks, creating interest when you land the first meeting, and continuing to add value so that you establish credibility as a business resource.

Case in point: in a recent meeting with the chief information officer of a Fortune 500 technology company, we asked, "Why would someone at your level ever agree to spend time with a salesperson?" The CIO's answer was simple:

> In my experience, professional salespeople offer me suggestions about solutions to business problems that even people in my own organization can't solve. Some of these salespeople have encountered similar problems in other organizations and have creatively addressed them. That's what I expect from salespeople who want to have a Trusted Advisor relationship with me.

In this simple answer is the code that will unlock almost everything you need to know about selling to executives.

First, this executive tells us that he expects salespeople to offer suggestions for his business instead of hearing the all-too-common "show up and throw up" sales pitch or a glad-hand social call. In today's wireless world, executives know more about your offering and your competitor's products than you can tell them in 60 minutes. They don't need a walking brochure, and if they want a friend, they can buy a dog. Instead, the CIO tells us to be professional, be conversant with the executive's business problems (or opportunities), and prepare a call plan that delivers some level of value to him.

As Gordon Gekko tells enthusiastic pitcher Bud Fox in Oliver Stone's film *Wall Street*: "You had what it took to get into my office, Sport; the question is, do you have what it takes to stay?"

Second, this CIO is saying that we'd better be prepared to tell him things he can't get from his own people, and that he wants to know how his business compares in the market. Is his company leading the curve, or is it falling behind? What do best practices look like? We need to know enough about how the executive's company does things today to be able to offer opinions about how it can do better. "You stop sending me information, and you start getting me some," was Gordon Gekko's next challenge to Bud Fox. "Surprise me." And so it is for us.

This CIO concludes with the ray of hope that a salesperson who is doing these things has a shot at standing out in the crowd. Note that he doesn't say that he wants a *vendor* relationship. His purchasing department can own those. What the executive is looking for is a *Trusted Advisor* relationship with salespeople who can speak on the executive's terms, discuss the same metrics, and add value to the thought process.

This second edition of *Selling to the C-Suite* is in response to three significant changes seen in selling and buying practices since this book's first edition.

First is the advent of social media platforms. When we ask salespeople where they go to learn about the executives on their hit lists, a popular answer is LinkedIn. When we ask them to flip the coin and tell us where they go to be seen by executives, it's also common to hear about LinkedIn blogs, plus e-mail marketing and Twitter. Yet when we look at actual usage statistics by executives, we see the 10 most popular apps ranked by monthly visitors are Facebook, YouTube, Instagram, Twitter, Reddit, Vine, Pinterest, Ask.fm, Tumblr, and Flickr. Coming in at 11th is Google+ and LinkedIn ranks 12th. YouTube has taken over from Facebook as the king of unique monthly visitors, yet the average attention span per video is only 40 seconds. The average CEO has 930 connections on LinkedIn, yet all LinkedIn users only average 17 minutes per month on the platform, and only 13 percent of millennials use it.[1]

A great many salespeople who think they've already conquered social media by using LinkedIn as their primary tool for reaching executive buyers may need to think again. The updated edition of this book gives clear direction.

Second is the fact that "digital natives" who grew up with technology have now joined the ranks of executives you're selling to. According to the U.S. Bureau of Labor Statistics, they now make up 35 percent of the adult workforce, and this trend is fairly consistent worldwide. They read (and also publish) opinions, reviews, and blogs about trends, products, and suppliers with an alacrity and speed that former executive ranks never did. Because they consume so much information and are connected to a variety of input sources, getting noticed by these executives against a wash of vanity posts and online noise requires a certain touch. Again, we show how in this new edition of the book.

Third, we see a rise in new ventures led by generation Y "millenipreneurs."[2] They're starting companies, failing faster, selling out quicker, managing larger headcounts, and targeting higher profits than the previous generation of baby boomers ever did. This shift is linked to new technology, but it's also the result of a cultural trend that accepts that you can be a CEO at a younger age, and fund your venture through nontraditional sources like crowdfunding and peer-to-peer lending platforms that require less security or equity than traditional sources like banks, venture capitalists, and angel investors.[3] It means there are now more executive buyers, at a younger age, with unique expectations about how you should sell to them.

Are you up to the challenge? Our invitation to you is to read on, find out where you rank, and learn how to climb the totem pole.

Now, start your engines . . .

Acknowledgments

For authors, the best part of completing a work is being able to acknowledge all of the people so important to the process. That begins with you, the amazing salesperson or sales executive now reading this book—the people who spend so much time on the road away from your families trying to "make something happen" in your company by generating orders for your company's products or services. The old adage, "Nothing happens until someone sells something," still holds true in the twenty-first century and that is the reason professional salespeople get out of bed every day. Thank you for doing what you do.

Every business book is a distillation of experiences and associations, and this one is no exception. We therefore thank our students, staff, and professional colleagues who have contributed in so many ways to the insights that make up this publication.

We acknowledge the collegial support of Jay E. Klompmaker, PhD, of the University of North Carolina; Alston Gardner, the visionary who founded Target Marketing Systems; and supporters from Hewlett-Packard who helped direct the 1995 "Selling to Senior Executives" initial study upon which some of our findings are based. In addition, Fred Burton and Nick Nascone from Target Marketing Systems provided many valuable insights.

Encouragement from the international community is always appreciated. Of particular note has been support from Kevin Wilson of the Sales Research Trust Ltd. UK; Lisa Napolitano, who headed the Strategic Account Management Association (SAMA) so well for so long; Steve Andersen of Performance Methods, Inc.; Anne An, former director of the Hewlett-Packard Business School in Beijing, China; and author Jerry Stapleton, whose ideas about becoming a true business resource are right on the money.

Of the many hundreds of sales professionals who have shared stories and anecdotes about selling to executives, we single out the unique personalities of Lee Bartlett, Dom DiMauro, Millard Allen, Alan Beck, Doug Boyle, Chuck Cagno, Jan Feddersen, Howard Freeman, John Harris, Helen Harwood, Karen Jackson, Bobby Knight, Ian Laidlaw, Matt Lovegrove, Lisa Nirell, Jeff Pace, Bruce Parkhurst, Stu Price, Jess Ray, Dennis Roberson, Spring Weng, Ronnie Wimberley, and our dear late friend Clare Sutton. The guidance and strong editorial contributions from our publishing team at McGraw-Hill led by Donya Dickerson and Cheryl Ringer transformed the manuscript into a comprehensive whole. We appreciate the insight, the talents, and the tremendous amount of work given to this book. Also, a thank you to John Outler for his assistance with many of the graphics.

Finally, our everlasting thanks to our spouses and children for putting up with our long hours and time on the road, in the air, and away from home during our sales careers.

Chapter 1

When Do Executives Get Involved in the Decision Process?

Selling to senior-level executives requires a different set of skills and strategies from the more traditional departmental-level transactional sale. Until the early 1980s, product was king. When a company introduced a new product, it was in many cases proprietary, allowing the company to get months or years of mileage of it being "best in class" or "leading edge" before a competitor leapfrogged it with an alternative offering.

Because of strong product differentiation, manufacturers dominated the business environment. For them, the standard go-to-market approach was a direct sales force, whose key functions were to provide basic product information, a point of contact with the vendor, and a human face to associate with the product. This sales force was typically made up of geographically assigned salespeople, each of whom called on a large number of accounts within a territory. They often sold to operations-level employees within individual departments like procurement or purchasing.

In the mid-1980s, priorities shifted. Customers were knowledgeable and comfortable with existing products and no longer needed a direct sales force to supply product information. Now they wanted low prices. Not altogether by coincidence, India and China stepped in as offshore providers of lower-cost manufacturing and services, and Western producers flocked to them in a bid to meet their customers' demands for savings while preserving their own margin. Supply Chain Management, Business Process Reengineering, Total Quality Management, and Six Sigma had their roots in this wave of stripping cost and inefficiency from the supply chain. The shift to lower-cost channels of distribution—or multichannel marketing—also began in this era, spawning hundreds of thousands of call centers, resellers, and online ordering portals.

At the same time, customers began to wonder how they could extract even more value from their suppliers, and they woke up to the fact that salespeople who were desperate to make a sale could be given the task of providing free consulting on ways to solve the more complex business problems. All of us who sold in that era needed knowledge of our own products, how they fit into our customer's operation, and how to assemble other components of a solution using products and services from third-party suppliers—we had to become solution architects and partner relationship managers, for whom selling a solution became a matter of juggling multiple relationships across our own company, the customer's company, and other vendors' companies. We were moving from the neat model of being a representative of one brand to being a broker for many products, services, and stakeholder agendas. To paraphrase from the tale of globalization that Thomas Friedman paints in *The Lexus and the Olive Tree* (HarperCollins, 1999): Sony moved from the stereo and CD market into the digital camera market where a 3.5-inch diskette became the film, the computer printer became the photo-processing store, and e-mail became the post office. Sony learned it could be Sony, Kodak, and Federal Express all at the same time as a one-stop business solution. Kodak responded to the challenge by promoting itself as a personal computer company. Compaq and Dell responded by saying computers were now commodities and they'd evolved to selling "business solutions." Accounting–consulting firms that had previously held business solutions as their bread and butter were less worried about the computer companies and more concerned by the likes of Goldman Sachs and other investment bankers that started selling tax and investment advice. You could read about these trends in books available at Borders stores, which now sold CDs—Sony's original market. Everyone is now in everyone else's business. Now even Borders is out of business, having closed its doors in 2011. Rival bookseller Barnes & Noble acquired Borders' trademarks and customer list.

That's the world of "business solutions," and by definition it demands that as salespeople, we move beyond the operations level and middle managers if we want to be heard above all the noise— we have to be more visible at the executive level.

In the 1990s another trend emerged. Business solutions that once seemed complicated to assemble, hence needed the input of salespeople to sort out the details, now became commonplace. Customers got the hang of them, identified the best vendors, and started compiling solutions themselves. The internal departments responsible for building these multivendor solutions started to get very good at it. Some of them were spun off as separate businesses, and one-stop-shop systems integration was born in the information technology market. The integrator ethos then spread in different forms to other industries.

Salespeople had educated the market on how to do it, and they were now competing with their very own customers for services work that had become more profitable than selling the product itself.

With the rise of Amazon, eBay, Alibaba, and other portals, the commoditization of high-value services and next day delivery accelerated. We remember not so many years ago people saying: "Okay, so we accept that customers can buy PCs over the Internet, but they'll never buy something as complicated as a server without seeing a rep!" Then came Dell, followed by a slew of others selling ever-more sophisticated products online. With information so freely available, transaction protocols so secure, and returns policies so lenient, there's almost no limit to the complexity of product that companies are willing to buy over the Internet. In an environment where buyers can conceive of, research, and complete procurement exercises totally online, salespeople need to work harder than ever to be seen as relevant.

This dilemma is compounded by an increase in competition brought on by modern online technology. In the twenty-first century we have inexpensive offshore production, crowdfunding, and peer-to-peer lending platforms to seed product and company development. With these, barriers to competition are reduced. Start-ups with new products, services, and niche expertise are cropping up at an increasing pace and chasing the same customers. This creates a noisy market that executives have learned to filter out. This makes getting on their radar even more of a challenge.

Forbes estimates that globally there are over a quarter million new product launches each year.[1] Invitations to learn about these hit the in-boxes of executive buyers at a rate of 96 e-mails a day,[2] of which 17 on average are weeded out as spam, and executive assistants patrol the rest. It's not surprising that recognition and recall are low.

In the current *Most Memorable New Product Launch* annual survey produced by Schneider Associates and Sentient Decision Science, a question is asked about how many people remember anything about new products they've just been introduced to:

- Baby boomers (born 1946–1964) recall 35 percent
- Gen X (born 1965–1976) recall 41 percent
- Gen Y Millennials (born 1977–1995) recall 49 percent
- Gen Z (born >1996) recall 61 percent, but only with repeat exposure in different sources[3]

The media sources that most impact product recall include:

- Television advertising = 60 percent
- Social media = 48 percent
- E-mail and YouTube = 24 percent
- A colleague's recommendation or search engines = 21 percent
- Print advertising = 15 percent

There is little difference in media response by gender, but there exists a clear generational gap. Gen Z and Gen Y leaders are much less likely than older executives to learn about new products through traditional information like TV commercials or paid-for media. These new generations binge-watch their favorite television shows and skip commercial breaks altogether. They're ad-resistant online as well, with a five-second trigger finger when ads pop up on YouTube and other sites they visit. Instead, the new generation of executives relies far more on personal referral, social media, and social proof from their trusted community than previous buyers. If you're not seen in the places they search for information when they're in the mood to find it, you'll find it difficult to break into the C-Suite in the next half-century.

BUILDING A FOUNDATION OF C-SUITE KNOWLEDGE

Recognizing that generational buying trends were changing as early as 1995, an Atlanta-based sales training company called Target Marketing Systems conducted a study in conjunction with Hewlett-Packard and the University of North Carolina's Kenan–Flagler Business School in Chapel Hill. This research was managed by Steve Bistritz, EdD (a coauthor of this book), who sought to discover what salespeople needed to do in the Internet age to remain relevant to senior executives, and what factors most influenced the executive decision-making process.

The original purpose of the research project was to examine not only how professional, business-to-business salespeople interacted and interfaced with C-level executives in client organizations, but to see how they built lasting, trust-based relationships with those executives. In addition, there was an interest in learning from the executive's perspective what salespeople had to do to deliver effective meetings. Coincidentally, at the same time Hewlett-Packard was attempting to establish a new national sales organization that would focus on selling to senior client executives, and the company genuinely wanted to understand what it took for those salespeople to gain the trust and credibility of those executives.

From its perspective, HP was trying to determine how its salespeople could be perceived as Trusted Advisors to client executives. The company decided to co-sponsor the study and did so by contributing to the cost and participating in the planning and execution of the study. It might be said that HP saw the researchers as Trusted Advisors and were prepared to coinvest in their work. As you'll see later in this book, it's possible to develop this type of relationship with your clients too, which unlocks budgets and relationships you seldom tap when your only engagement is around your standard list of products and services.

The rationale for Target Marketing Systems to cosponsor the study was that the company was in the midst of developing an instructor-led workshop for professional salespeople on selling to executives and was interested in determining the best ways for salespeople to create, maintain, and leverage relationships with senior-level executives in client organizations. In perusing sales journals and the existing literature in 1995, few articles were written by C-level executives discussing their relationships with professional salespeople or why they would want to meet with new salespeople attempting a first contact. At that time, most books and articles on this topic were written by salespeople about their anecdotal experience dealing with senior client executives. The literature did not speak about creating and establishing those relationships from the *executive's* perspective.

Interest developed at the University of North Carolina's Business School because a professor of marketing at the school, Dr. Jay Klompmaker, was a member of the advisory board at Target Marketing Systems. He saw the research project as an outstanding opportunity for four of his graduate students in the MBA program—all of whom had previous experience as business-to-business salespeople—to participate in a practical study that could make a significant contribution to the profession. Their participation subsequently became part of the practicum requirements for the MBA. Dr. Klompmaker duplicated the literature search and reached an identical conclusion about the lack of empirical information in this field.

Preparation for the executive interviews took nearly six months; a detailed questionnaire was developed, a list of potential executives to be interviewed was created, and practice interviews were conducted. The executives interviewed came from the client bases of Target Marketing Systems and Hewlett-Packard. The executives were not prescreened in any manner, except that each needed to be willing to commit an hour of their time, and had to function at the vice president or CXO level. Purchasing and procurement executives were specifically excluded from the survey.

The experienced sales professionals on the MBA track at UNC practiced with HP executives, then interviewed more than 60 client executives, ranging from vice presidents to chairpersons. Interviews were conducted in person or by telephone and lasted up to 60 minutes. The reason for conducting interviews in this manner was to make certain that all responses came directly from the executives themselves. If we had sent an executive our questionnaire on this topic, it may have been completed by the executive's assistant or a lower-level manager and would have compromised the process. We also wanted to capture anecdotal comments from executives. These goals could most likely be achieved in face-to-face or telephone interviews.

Executives were selected from diverse industries, including transportation, textiles, telecommunications, utilities, financial services, technology, printing, and office furniture. Four years later, in the spring of 1999, the same study was expanded in collaboration with the Center for Business and Industrial Marketing at Georgia State University in Atlanta, with more than 125 senior executives surveyed in total.

In preparing for the initial interviews with executives, Hewlett-Packard arranged for each of the four MBA students to conduct a series of practice interviews with some of HP's own senior executives. These in-person practice interviews took place at HP's corporate headquarters in California. The purpose of these practice interviews was to carefully vet the questionnaire that had been developed, make certain that there were no questions that could be misinterpreted or issues that could arise, and also confirm that the MBA students were thoroughly prepared to conduct effective 60-minute interviews with client executives.

To ensure that the process was conducted appropriately, the research manager accompanied the MBA students to each of the practice interviews to validate the process and help set the tone for each interview. We also wanted to verify that each of the four MBA students was prepared, confident, and competent, because their next step was a live interview with a senior-level client executive. These initial interviews were very successful and provided us with additional insight into how to conduct the interviews with client executives, as well as how to treat the executives during the process. The executives at HP who participated in the practice interviews also told us that the process provided value to them because they gained additional insight into how they could perhaps work more effectively with the salespeople they dealt with on an ongoing basis.

To test for cultural variance, the research was expanded in 2005 by Nic Read (this book's other coauthor), who at the time was president of the sales consulting firm SalesLabs and an advisor to the Hewlett-Packard Business School in Beijing, China. Hewlett-Packard again proved invaluable in the research process. Its business school in China, in concert with Ivy League universities, provided Executive MBA programs to Chinese executives. Over a two-year period, when executives and senior managers finished a course of study, they were asked to complete a detailed questionnaire about how they viewed China's entry into the World Trade Organization in terms of the challenges it created for local companies, the implications for them as leaders, and what they looked for from the salespeople and vendors who were knocking on China's door with new solutions. The research team collected surveys and interviewed more than 400 chairpersons, vice presidents, and managing directors of Chinese state-owned enterprises and multinational companies in the insurance, biotech, pharmaceutical, telecommunications, banking, airline, steel, and information technology industries. A number of respondents came from regional neighbors that included Taiwan, Japan, South Korea, the Philippines, Thailand, Indonesia, Malaysia, Singapore, and Australia. This study lifted the total sample of executives who were interviewed to more than 500, from which surprisingly consistent findings were extrapolated on how executives get involved in the buying cycle, regardless of culture, and what salespeople need to do to gain their trust and create value.

The following sections reveal what we learned.

EXECUTIVE INVOLVEMENT IN THE BUYING CYCLE

Salespeople who want to build relationships with executives must enter the picture early in the buying cycle because this is when 80 percent of executives usually become involved in significant purchase decisions (see Figure 1.1).

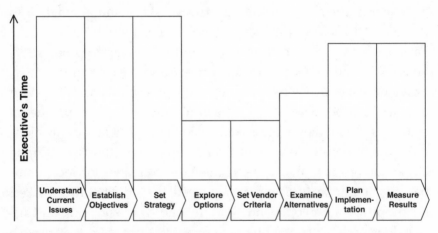

Figure 1.1 Executive Involvement in the Buying Cycle

The executives' motivation at this stage is to understand current business issues, establish project objectives, and set the overall project strategy to deal with what might be termed a *breakthrough initiative*: something that is critical to the client's success because of significant payback from its implementation or serious consequences if action is delayed or not taken.

According to one executive from the office furniture industry:

I get involved in the "what" and "why," not so much the "how." At the beginning, I put in a lot of personal time making sure the project's on the right track and moving in the right direction.

Another executive from the airline industry told us:

I'm planning now for how my business will look 10 years from now. It's difficult to forecast on our own, so we depend on the ideas of suppliers and partners in the same industry, on the belief that separately we might be wrong, but together we're probably right. Vendors who can't engage in that forward thinking don't get off the ground with me.

Comments regarding executive involvement in the early phase of the buying cycle were consistent in each of our three studies.

During the middle phase of the buying cycle, executives tend to reduce their involvement and delegate decisions to subordinates or committees. Executives in the survey said that once a clear vision is set, it's time to empower the people below them. "Once we've defined the parameters, my tendency is to get out of the way," said one respondent. Most of the executives never or only occasionally involve themselves at this stage.

However, all three research studies confirmed that executives get significantly involved once again late in the buying cycle to evaluate whether the vendors can really deliver the original vision and to measure the results of the implementation. They want to understand whether the vendor delivered the value that was originally committed to. They also told us that the closer they get to the contract being awarded, the less likely they are to supersede the recommendations of the evaluation team; the purchasing decision has usually already been made in their minds, if not on paper.

Do you see the problem here?

The middle-to-late phase of the buying cycle is the period when senior executives in medium-size to large companies are *least likely* to open their calendar to a salesperson. But this is when most invitations to quote and submit proposals happen. Salespeople who get their first scent of a deal at this stage and expect to "meet the boss" are usually frustrated by the difficulty of doing so. If you are able to gain access to the right executive early enough in the buying process, your efforts are likely to be rewarded. But don't expect marketing to line up those meetings for you. Here's why.

Executives are increasingly using the Internet to inform their views, but they do not search on the category of solution because, this early in the process, they're not educated enough to know where a solution will come from. Instead, they search based on the problem confronting them. This is a challenge for marketers if their search engine optimization program uses only tag words that describe their solution (which is most of them).

Try this experiment. Imagine that you are an executive and you're early in your buying cycle. You don't know what the solution will be yet, but you know that your problems are "customer growth" and "declining revenue." You want to see who can solve those problems.

Key these two phrases into a search engine and write down the top three hits for each. Here's what we found doing this experiment on Google:

"customer growth": 326,000,000 hits

1. An in-app analytics software company
2. A professional services company
3. A direct mail company

The top three hits for this problem reach very different types of vendors talking about their products and services. This doesn't add value to an executive who wants to explore a specific business problem and isn't ready to home in on a solution.

"declining revenue": 45,500,000 hits

1. A 2017 *BusinessInsider* news article about a software company in decline
2. A 2017 *Forbes* news article about a beverage company in decline
3. A 2017 *USA Today* news article about an online review company in decline

The top three hits for this problem led to news stories by journalists about companies facing declining revenue. So did the next 70 hits. It wasn't until the eighth screen of this query that the first potential supplier of services weighed in with an opinion. Let's face it, nobody clicks eight screens deep.

This exercise shows why so many salespeople don't get invited to talk to executives early on—when executives are looking for ideas about solving their problems, most companies that offer answers can't be found. The reason is that when marketing teams create search engine listings and meta tags, the phrases they use are focused on how the seller sees the world (all about the product), not how the executive buyer sees it (all about the problem).

Let's put this hypothesis to the test. Do the same experiment again, but this time let's think like one of those marketing people who can't see beyond their product (which, as we'll discuss in the next chapter, is most of them). Let's choose the well-worn product categories of "customer relationship management" and "account management" as solutions that would be a good fit for the previously cited problems of "customer growth" and "declining revenue," and see if the search result shows a tighter grouping:

"customer relationship management": 17,000,000 hits

1. A CRM software company
2. A CRM software company
3. A CRM software company

"account management": 33,000,000 hits

1. A scholarly article by a sales training company
2. A scholarly article by a sales training company
3. A scholarly article by a sales training company

Look at the comparison. We see 584,000 hits when our executive is first exploring these problems and is most open to new ideas (early in the buying cycle). But as we've seen, most of these hits failed to connect to relevant sellers. It's only after the buyer is already educated about a product category (usually the middle of the buying process, when executives are *least likely* to be involved) that most Internet marketing connects buyers to sellers, in this case 50,000,000 of them who were marketing their wares using product-speak, not customer-speak. Ever wondered why so many evaluators have already pigeonholed you before your first meeting? Or why so few executive prospects spend their time camping on your doorstep? Now you know.

While writing this book we attended an enormous marketing event staged by a major business intelligence software company. A record number of prospects, customers, partners, and media representatives attended. The company had spent real money on this event, and it showed. Anticipation built as huge screens counted down to the opening address, punctuated by spinning lights and rock music. When the vice president of marketing mounted the stage, he delivered a passionate presentation about how his company was redefining its industry, and how its customers were no longer satisfied being sold a bunch of widgets; they wanted solutions to their business problems. Our curiosity was piqued by the expectation that we were about to see a company make the leap to true customer-centricity.

The vice president revealed the next slide, which showed the company's products grouped into neat boxes, and declared they were now going to market several preconfigured solutions to make selection easier, labeled in industry-speak.

We didn't hear the rest of his speech. Instead we sat pondering why it is that so many companies come so close to getting it right, then choke. This company was clearly on the right path, but it was no more than one step away from pushing its product, despite dressing it up with the word *solution* 26 times, before we zoned out. To truly focus on solutions means to solve problems. To talk about problems is to abandon the self-indulgence of promoting our products. This is not a comfortable place for most marketers. Which is why next year, when this company runs the same event, it will probably be attended by the same gearheads attracted by shiny toys described in product-speak, and never be discovered by executives who are searching in customer-speak.

All three of our C-Suite research studies told us that 80 percent of executives get involved early in their buyer's journey to prioritize projects and set the vision. We know they use the Internet to explore options for solving their problem. And we've seen that most companies fail to position themselves around problems, so don't get on the executive's radar early enough.

This means that unless your marketing machine changes its approach to lead generation (which we discuss in the next chapter), you need to rely on good old-fashioned prospecting and selling

Executive's View of	Stage 1	Stage 2	Stage 3	Stage 4
Your Objective	Make a Sale	Make a Contribution	Provide Insight	Provide Leverage
Your Contribution to the Company	Disruption to the Executive's Business Day	Logical Thinker	Critical Thinker	Strategic Resource
Your Relationship with the Executive	Intermittent	Interactive	Interesting	Interdependent
Your Status	Commodity Supplier	Emerging Resource	Problem Solver	Trusted Advisor
Access to the Executive	Sent Down	Considered	Occasional	Continual

Figure 1.2 Four Stages of Sales Proficiency

skills to reach executives early in their buying cycle. To pull that off, you need sales proficiency that's beyond the capabilities of most salespeople.

But you can learn it.

There are four stages of sales proficiency that you may pass through during your sales career (see Figure 1.2).

FOUR STAGES OF SALES PROFICIENCY
1. Commodity Supplier

Salespeople who are Commodity Suppliers see the world through a pair of product glasses. They believe that if they can just get the opportunity to show their product or service, the features of their product or their brand will help them succeed. Their world extends little further than the execution of tactics such as setting up meetings, making sales presentations, giving demonstrations, and writing proposals. As a result, they rarely get involved early enough in a sale to create opportunities with an executive buyer.

We participated in a conference call between one such salesperson who was attempting to make a sale and a Symantec vice president in California. The sales rep boasted before the call: "I don't need to know their business, their issues, or anything about them. We've got the best product on the market, and that speaks for itself." To his credit, when we suggested that he might prepare for the call by at least checking the firm's website for the latest news, he spent a few minutes browsing. However, to our chagrin, his first words were: "So what's this new initiative I see listed all over your website? It looks like this S-Y-M-C project is pretty important!" The salesperson didn't know SYMC is Symantec's stock market symbol!

This rep's belief that product is king was so deeply entrenched that he never felt the need to understand the client's world and believed that clients existed only to help him meet his quota. Those operations-level customers who agreed to see him considered this rep nothing more than the guy to call when they needed a discount on an order that they'd already decided to place. They also knew that he'd always buy the drinks when they had people in town, so they would regularly dent his expense account under the guise of *account management*. Consequently, he was one of the highest-selling yet least profitable salespeople in his company.

The executives we interviewed typically called this type of salesperson a "product expert," and one that they would rarely waste their time on. One said: "If all someone can do is talk features, functions, and benefits, then he's going to turn me off pretty fast." Another complained: "At the end of these meetings, I feel like I was interrupted, that they wasted my time."

Many executives indicated that they would immediately refer these salespeople to either executives or staff members at lower levels of the organization who can deal with the product and technical issues that the senior-level executives perceive to be the only issues that these Commodity Suppliers are comfortable discussing.

While, through diligence and consistent efforts, the salesperson who has a Commodity Supplier relationship may have been able to schedule an initial meeting with an executive, her inability to discuss the issues that are critical to executives converts an extraordinary opportunity into wasted time for both the executive and the salesperson. At that point, the salesperson's ability to gain further access to the same senior-level executive becomes questionable, at best.

Salespeople typically only get one shot at impressing an executive, and Commodity Suppliers seldom score a second appointment. However, tactics that the salesperson can implement at this point are worth mentioning. To demonstrate some level of follow-through that might impress the executive, a salesperson should do two things to try to secure another meeting with him, namely, (1) ask the executive for an introduction to the appropriate lower-level person, and (2) ask the executive for a follow-on meeting to review the results.

Asking the executive for an introduction to the lower-level executive or staff person shows the person at the lower level the importance of the meeting, and asking the senior-level executive for a follow-up meeting may represent one way for the salesperson to secure return access.

However, don't feel we're saying that this type of selling is wrong. Commodity Suppliers have their place under the right circumstances. As former General Electric CEO Jack Welch said: "You can't grow long-term if you can't eat short-term." Selling like a Commodity Supplier on deals where the customer has a fast buying cycle is exactly the right thing to do. These deals don't need to be overengineered; they need to be closed before the competition finds them. A dozen small deals now is better than any large deal in the future.

2. Emerging Resource

A salesperson who is an Emerging Resource might get involved in a company's decision process after being tested as a

Commodity Supplier for some time, typically at an operations or middle-management level. These people have earned their spurs and won the right to do more work as a result of their track record.

Becoming an Emerging Resource is the result of a negotiation process in which Commodity Suppliers sell their value beyond pure product to other services and resources that they bring to the relationship. Once customers are convinced of this value, they grant the Emerging Resource the type of contract that keeps competitors out of an account and widens the "license to hunt" for a specified time in return for preferential pricing or service. This is the same principle seen in politics when nations ratify their relationship by signing trade agreements that confer "preferred trading partner" status on one or both parties. It's based on the perception that transacting with Emerging Resources is less risky and lower cost than receiving submissions from countless unknown suppliers each time a need arises.

Emerging Resources stand out from Commodity Suppliers when they do their homework to identify what advantages can be created for the customer by awarding preference to a single supplier. This has to be more than a generic value proposition. It's based on knowing how the customer orders and who else the customer trades with and being able to spot the inefficiencies that having a single one-stop vendor can solve. It's also about having the patience to build credentials in small ways to earn the right to pitch this proposition and get credit as a logical thinker.

3. Problem Solver

It's at the Problem Solver level of sales proficiency that salespeople shift from an internal focus on their products to an external focus on the customer's wider world. As a result, they start to see and talk about issues that aren't immediately connected to a current deal, but are yet to be handled. Problem Solvers seek an approach that will solve business problems and shift their gaze away from their own product long enough to listen to the customer and understand the larger environment within which the product must operate. Their ideas are usually forward-looking and more strategic, which qualifies them to meet with executives who are looking to the same horizon for answers.

Executives have a better opinion of Problem Solvers than they do of Commodity Suppliers and Emerging Resources. They describe a Problem Solver salesperson as: "Someone who is a potential resource. During the presentation, we explored several creative ideas together. I'll take these ideas under consideration and possibly meet with him again."

4. Trusted Advisor

Many salespeople plateau at the Problem Solver level, so how can you stand out in a pack of other Problem Solvers? Become a Trusted Advisor by focusing on the value of your personal relationship with the executive. You develop this relationship by understanding the executive as a person first, then recognizing the executive's broad vision for his or her business. You advise on the common obstacles to avoid, suggest proven best practices, and build relationships within the political dynamic of the executive's inner circle, that is, those trusted lieutenants inside and outside of the company who the executive turns to for advice. They serve as a compass and a mine detector by providing insight and foresight that the executive isn't already tapped into.

Executives in our studies repeatedly cited the continuing value of dealing with salespeople who had obviously helped solve similar business problems for other customers. It was common to hear: "Some of these salespeople can relate to business problems at a very high level. They understand that their solution may not be a panacea, but they deliver business value by helping me explore various options. My objective is to discuss my business problems with them and develop realistic solutions, not to see a slick sales presentation."

Another executive cited the salesperson's ability to draw on internal or even external partner resources as a way of possibly solving a problem as a key indicator of business value. She said, "The salesperson I meet with should provide me with the benefit of his experience, but also be able to secure the additional resources required to provide a broader view of the solution."

Salespeople who operate at the Trusted Advisor level of a business relationship with multiple executives in several organizations quickly develop skills that can be transferred from customer to customer. Senior-level executives in those organizations immediately recognize the salespeople who regularly connect with executives at their level because they can sense the business knowledge, confidence, and competence that those salespeople demonstrate. It's as if the executives have a sixth sense and can spot the salespeople who are continually dealing with their peers in other organizations.

Of all of the traits demonstrated, being prepared for a meeting with the executive is most highly valued and quickly recognized. There is no substitute for having a substantial understanding of the customer's industry, their company, and the customer's executives themselves. Developing this insight into the customer is also one of the easiest ways to develop a genuine and lasting rapport with senior-level executives. This knowledge enables you to be in a better position to serve as a consultant to the customer, contributing your insights and creating the foundation for a long-term, collaborative relationship. Such demonstrations of business knowledge are observed to help convert what might otherwise be ordinary meetings into extraordinary opportunities, where you gain continued access to the executive and shorten your sales cycle.

One executive described a Trusted Advisor salesperson as: "Someone I consider a business consultant who gave me ideas about my business that even my own people didn't come up with. As a result, I felt we had a business meeting where she demonstrated some compelling business value and also gave me some reasons why I should grant her continued access to me."

This continued access to senior executives is critical to building the long-term relationships required to consistently succeed. Trusted Advisor salespeople don't wait to jump in at the middle of the buying cycle, which is when Commodity Supplier salespeople first get alerted to a deal—they get involved earlier to help the client identify and assess options, then determine the most effective way to address his high-priority issues.

A famous deal by NBC illustrates what it takes to be a Trusted Advisor.

The broadcast rights to the Olympic Games are usually awarded in four-year packages, one Olympics at a time. NBC, ABC, Fox, and other broadcasters routinely compete in that four-year cycle to win the coveted contract. But NBC's Dick Ebersol blew that model out of the water by locking up the broadcast rights for both Sydney in 2000 and Salt Lake City in 2002, followed quickly by a second deal for all Olympic coverage through to Beijing in 2008. It was an unprecedented deal in broadcasting history. *Sports Illustrated* magazine featured an excellent article on Ebersol's deal in its Christmas Day edition in 1995. Here are a few outtakes that explain key principles by which Trusted Advisors like Ebersol operate:

- Trusted Advisors determine what the object of their affection wants to hear. They know what these people want to hear because they are consistently better prepared and better informed than their rivals. "Ebersol rises at 6:15 every morning and reads four daily newspapers."
- Trusted Advisors know the personal agendas of their customers and find ways to *leverage their company's resources* to deliver what their customers want. "Ebersol came up with an offer to

broadcast a weekly Olympic magazine show from 1996 to 2002. He knew coverage in non-Olympic years held appeal for Juan Antonio Samaranch" (then the president of the International Olympic Committee). Ebersol changed the rules of the game and, in effect, moved the goal posts.

- Trusted Advisors listen for little clues. "Samaranch congratulated Ebersol on the 'stability' they had achieved and on the 'partnership' they had forged. Ebersol was struck by Samaranch's repeated references to the long-term nature of their relationship" and sensed that his customer might be interested in a much longer-term contract than the two Olympics already signed up.
- Trusted Advisors create deals that offer personal value as well as sound commercial value, and they do so in a way that makes the buyer and the seller *interdependent*. Ebersol came up with what was nicknamed the Sunset Project—a deal for not two but five Olympic Games that created long-term financial stability for the IOC and a legacy for Samaranch to leave behind.

As one Trusted Advisor salesperson explained: "Instead of just reacting to a customer's request for a quote, I start becoming more inquisitive about why the customer may want something and the eventual effects of buying my product or service."

Being "inquisitive" the way this Trusted Advisor suggests means understanding the executive's current issues and helping him establish objectives for his broad business interests before setting a strategy to explore external capabilities you can bring to bear. To make that happen, you need to do your homework on the customer, his business, and his industry.

Where do you rank? What do you need to do differently to advance? It's food for thought.

CHAPTER SUMMARY

Let's summarize what we've discussed in this chapter about the first question in our research: "When do executives get involved in the buying process?" Let's break it down to the top three messages:

1. *Get in early.* Executives get involved in purchasing decisions early, when the original vision is being set and before the task of finding suppliers is delegated. They use the Internet to inform their thought process about the problem they face. Most marketing fails to help them find you at this stage, so you need to rely on your selling skills. However, if your marketing department sends out problem-focused messages that attract the executives who face those problems, and sends a series of repetitive wake-up calls to help them recognize that (a) they have a problem and (b) you can solve that problem, then your ability to plug into the start of the executive decision process will improve.

2. *Focus on their breakthrough initiative.* Use your knowledge of the executive's business drivers to identify her *breakthrough initiative*—the single most important problem or opportunity she needs to invest in where your products or services can make a demonstrable difference. Breakthrough initiatives are typically identified only at the executive level, meaning that people at lower levels of the organization may not even be aware of them until they are formalized as a project. By the time they become formal and other suppliers are invited to bid, the executive's views of both solution and vendor have often already been set if one supplier has demonstrated thought leadership from the start.

3. *Meet with executives to measure the results of the implementation.* Our research told us that senior-level executives want to meet with salespeople and review the value that the salespeople's solutions have delivered to their organization—so take advantage of that opportunity. Don't assume that executives always have a clear understanding of the value you delivered—make certain you communicate that value directly to them in a succinct manner. In addition, consider conducting annual meetings with senior-level executives to review the value you deliver to them on a recurring basis. This could elevate their view of you to either Problem Solver or Trusted Advisor status.

Chapter 2

Marketing to the C-Suite

In the previous chapter, we established that, as salespeople strive to retain profitable customers and win new ones, they need to gain access to and establish credibility with senior executives. These stakeholders are often among the first to see that an opportunity exists to improve their operation through the purchase of external goods and services. In small- and medium-size companies, this same person may stay on as project leader or serve on the evaluation committee. But in large enterprises, the executive may see their job as complete when they've handed over the task of selecting a supplier to the purchasing officer. After that happens, the ability of a salesperson to connect with the executive who initiated a project may be restricted by the person to whom the task is delegated.

Good salespeople know that if their first entry into a deal is through a formal request for proposal (RFP), or tender, they've already lost the upper hand. They attempt to counter the tender process by offering the quid pro quo of providing the requested documentation in return for interviews with key people, accompanied by the suggestion that by doing so, they'll be better able to prepare a solution that meets all the buyer's needs. This sounds good on the surface, but purchasing managers tell us that, under the terms of a tender process (especially when selling to government agencies), if they grant this dispensation to one vendor, they must do so for all or risk the appearance of playing favorites—a matter of corporate probity. Purchasers also point out that when salespeople ask to meet other stakeholders, what they really hear is: "I want to interview people to determine your needs because you probably didn't scope this for me to win" or "I want to build a base of supporters because I don't believe you will buy from me except under political duress." How perceptive.

It is therefore not surprising to hear buyers make the legitimate request that we route all communication through them and not call over their heads. We should also not be surprised that by the time we get invited to the party, much of the buying process has already been completed, with buyers using the Internet to window-shop, create a short list, and make comparisons.

International Data Corporation (IDC) estimates that nearly 50 percent of the purchasing process for complex solutions is completed before companies engage with supplier salespeople,[1] even when a supplier contacted is an incumbent. It's revelatory that 75 percent of all B2B buyers and 84 percent of C-Suite executives use social media to help them make purchasing decisions today.

You can see in Figure 2.1 what 760 executives from across industries revealed about their top four sources for opinions and information as they pass through the early, middle, and late stages of a buying process. Since the previous edition of this book, a recommendation from third parties they trust has always ranked

INFORMATION SOURCE	EARLY	MIDDLE	LATE
Industry-specific media	1	2	6
Third-party expert recommendations	4	1	2
Professional social networks (e.g., LinkedIn)	8	4	1
Search engine	2	3	10
Microblogs (e.g., Twitter)	3	13	5
General word of mouth	5	8	8
In-person events (e.g., meetings and phone calls)	6	9	12
Supplier websites	7	6	11
Supplier content (e.g., white papers and infographics)	9	5	7
General media	10	10	13
Personal social networks (e.g., Facebook)	11	11	4
Private domain or topic specific	12	7	3
Digital events (e.g., webinar or virtual meeting)	13	12	9

Figure 2.1 Information Sources That Influence Executive Buying by Stage of Sale

(IDC Social Buying Study, February 2014.)

high, and we see it still does. However, we now see a rise in the importance of "social proof" (where the opinions of many people are aggregated, also called "the wisdom of crowds") and how executives are now comfortable accepting the opinions of people who may be strangers, but who belong to a tribe they trust on social networks, blogs, and even search engines.

Knowing this may cause you to ponder if you or your company are visible and being talked about in these social forums. If not, it's an area to get active in, because if your C-Suite buyers are going there for information about you, your competitors, and the value of your solutions, you need to find a way to have a voice in the discussions they see there.

New York Times columnist Thomas Friedman called the Internet "the democratization of information." In his book *The Lexus and the Olive Tree* (HarperCollins, 1999), Friedman cites *USA Today*'s technology columnist Kevin Maney as saying:

> As a world-changing invention, the net echoes many of the characteristics of the printing press. It brings a dramatic drop in the cost of creating, sending, and storing information while vastly increasing its availability. It breaks information monopolies.

It's these "information monopolies" that salespeople have depended on for leverage in the buyer-seller relationship since selling began. The Internet is a counterstroke to the customer's dependence on salespeople for information, especially at the executive level.

How did this happen?

In the late 1990s, marketing started getting the hang of web coding and packed websites full of information about their company's credentials, product information, customer testimonials, and even its rate cards. Marketing didn't realize it at the time, but these websites were stripping away what had formerly been a large part of a salesperson's role as a knowledge provider. Because of the *info-glut* on most corporate websites, many customers no longer needed the diagnosis of a salesperson—they could self-medicate.

A problem many sales pros encounter today is that the majority of prospects aren't actively searching. They have latent or chronic problems, but they've learned to live with them, and need to be awakened to the fact that a better way exists. Without this awakening, they have no interest in a salesperson's solutions. According to Vorsight, at any given time only 4 percent of your market is actively buying, 40 percent are ready to start looking at options, and 56 percent aren't ready or don't have a current need.[2] Marketing departments today don't generally pump out material designed to turn a buyer who has learned to cope with a chronic problem into one who feels an acute and urgent need to change (which is what much of B2B selling requires). No, most marketing works to connect to and convert the low-hanging fruit of customers already searching for products and services. But it wasn't always this way.

Modern marketing began with the printing press in the fifteenth century. The first newspapers sold space for print advertising, which was extended to direct mail and mail-order catalogs in the 1850s. In the 1920s, radio was invented, and companies sponsored shows in return for their products being mentioned. This same format was used when television shows went on the air in the 1940s. With few exceptions, the products being pitched through print and electronic media were all household consumer goods like soap powder, toothpaste, deodorant, apparel, kitchenware, food and beverages, travel, and automobiles.

Today's consumer goods exist in well-defined product categories. Customers know what the product is and what it does, and the decision to buy is based on personal preferences concerning its style, taste, price, prestige, utility, or novelty. Marketing of these products focuses less on "why do I need it?" and more on "which one should I buy?" because consumers are already educated about the product category and the value of using it. Choosing between Brand A and Brand B is therefore the impulse that marketing typically targets.

But in the century between 1850 and 1950, industrialization was inventing products that had never existed before. These goods were not in categories that consumers were familiar with, and their value wasn't as self-evident. For example, today's consumer doesn't think twice about buying a refrigerator. Yet in 1932, Electrolux had to run advertisements to convince people that they needed to stop storing perishable food in an ice cellar and put a gas-powered refrigerator inside their kitchen instead.

The Electrolux advertisement in Figure 2.2 shows a woman wearing horse blinders, with the headline, "Blinders . . . because she shies at new ideas." The copy opens with: "Flying machines, horseless carriages—they had their skeptics. . . . All we ask is that you go and see Electrolux with your eyes wide open."

The image and headline imply the following messages:

- To the husbands of the time: "If your wife resists change, in the age of the horseless carriage, she is like a horse with blinders on."
- To the wives of the time: "If you don't move with the times, your husband might trade you in for a faster model."

The content is politically incorrect by today's standards. Yet the marketing technique was perfect:

- The product was unknown to its target market, so pitching features and benefits to people who weren't yet convinced that they needed the product at all would fall on deaf ears.
- To attract buyers for the first time, marketers talked about a problem they knew members of their target market identified with.

Figure 2.2 "New" Product Marketing Using Shame as a Motivator

Source: Good Housekeeping, 1932.

THE THREE DOORS OF MARKETING

The first salvo for marketing household consumer goods when those goods were previously unknown was to talk about a problem, make people aware they had the problem, and gain their interest in finding a solution—which opened their minds to the concept of making a change and spending money. These marketing activities were called a *Door Opener*.

The second salvo came once prospects recognized they had the problem. Either marketing or a sales agent reinforced the message of how bad the pain was and suggested there was a way to avoid that pain. With hope kindled, a call to action was offered to buy the product. This was called a *Door Closer*.

Door Openers and Door Closers were delivered in newspapers, magazines, and other publications, as well as on radio and television. Sometimes the Door Closer was at the point of sale in a showroom, over the telephone, on the doorstep, in the lounge room, or over the counter.

The third and final salvo came after prospects became customers. Marketing exposed customers to a different stream of advertisements that showed happy and successful people benefiting from the product and using add-ons that added to their enjoyment. This reinforced what a wise decision it was to buy, showed social proof that the buyer belonged to a club of other satisfied customers, and offered new options to keep customers locked-in to the brand. This was called the *Revolving Door*.

This three-step marketing model (see Figure 2.3) worked like a dream for the *marketing of unfamiliar product categories* invented from the 1930s to the 1990s. By the turn of the millennium most new products were offshoots of categories already well understood. They represented an evolution rather than a revolution. As a result, marketing in traditional media has become a game of brand preference and market share. Door Openers aren't needed there. Most messaging is a Door Closer or Revolving Door. Yet we see an

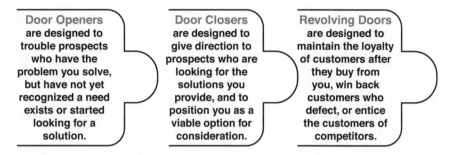

Figure 2.3 Classic Three-Step Marketing Model of the Early 1900s

interesting corollary to all three doors in the way online marketing campaigns are now run. With the Internet allowing sellers to connect to billions of people who don't know them, their brand, their products, or their value, Door Openers are back in fashion.

E-mail marketing linked to campaign-specific landing pages and websites has taken the place of press advertising to introduce the concept of a problem, make people aware they have it, and make them interested in finding a solution (the Door Opener).

Once convinced a problem exists, customers can explore it online in a single click of the e-mail link that brings them to your website and the various offers you make there to convey information or extend a call to action, such as to download a paper, participate in a survey, join a webinar, or talk to a salesperson (the Door Closer).

Other e-mails are designed to share best practices about the product or service purchased; offer insights and how-to tips; promote training workshops, add-ons, and other products; and overall create a sense of belonging in a community and stickiness (the Revolving Door).

The tools have changed. The model stays the same.

But unless you are offering a product that can be purchased on the spot, or are dealing with a business customer near the end of their "buyer's journey" (hence they're ready to act), most prospects will leave a website they've been enticed to visit through e-mail without taking action on the first visit.

Next, the customer will most typically open a query in a search engine about the problem they now identify with. This takes them to other vendors' websites that talk about the problem your marketing convinced them they have. Here they get exposed to the Door Openers of other vendors in the guise of sidebars or banner ads and headlines (does your website appear in their search and reinforce your prominence?), plus the opinions of parties on forums that provide social proof about how bad the problem can be if not eliminated, ways they solved the problem, and which vendors do the best work (do you have actual customers or even hired agents from Fiverr or freelancer.com writing on your behalf on social forums?).

These inputs go into the buyer's mental hopper to gauge if the problem appears to be something others are focusing on, if it's severe enough to spend time and money on now, and which suppliers look like they have answers. If you appear favorably in the places they search, you increase your chances of engagement.

DON'T WAIT FOR MARKETING TO CREATE YOUR LEADS

As a salesperson of the twenty-first century, you can't afford to wait for your marketing department to create leads for you. The years 1995 to 2015 were marked by the introduction and refinement of e-commerce, CRM systems, and online marketing. These technologies were managed by IT and marketing departments, and over two decades the sales activity of "demand creation" shifted ever further outside the sales department. It's not uncommon today for salespeople to do almost no prospecting, but be measured on their ability to convert marketing leads into appointments and sales.

On the surface it looks like a fine arrangement: salespeople who don't enjoy prospecting don't need to, and marketing delivers a steady stream of qualified leads for the salesperson to turn into revenue. Idyllic.

Yet this may have led to a generation of salespeople whose prospecting skills are in atrophy. This would be acceptable if prospecting were only a onetime event, easily handed to marketing. But the same skills are needed elsewhere, such as when networking across a key account to open doors, or reaching multiple members of an evaluation team to win a large sales opportunity. It's our observation that deemphasizing a B2B salesperson's responsibility for prospecting at the top of the funnel (where they get the most practice) can limit a rep's ability to draw on those same skills further down the funnel (where they practice less regularly).

Research from CEB Inc. (formerly the Corporate Executive Board) indicates an average of 5.4 decision makers is *always* involved in B2B purchasing decisions.[3] Gartner, Inc. suggests up to six additional people can *occasionally* be added based on their subject matter expertise or relevance of their formal role.[4] Yet examinations of opportunity plans, CRM registers, and deal reviews reveal that salespeople seem reluctant to call on more than four people in a single sales opportunity today, compared to an average of seven people a decade ago.[5] We conclude from this that not only are prospecting and networking skills in decline today, but sellers are attempting to connect to too few people in the sales they're working.

When a deal review shows a need to network more widely and start calling outside their comfort zone, the average salesperson makes only two attempts to reach a new person, with 44 percent giving up after the first attempt if not successful. Yet executives report that unless introduced to a salesperson by someone on their team, it can take up to six attempts to reach them.[6] Here we see another gap between the effort given and what's really needed.

We mention this because it's time for salespeople to take back control of their prospecting.

Executive buyers have grown resistant to mass marketing messages in their in-box. Messaging intent on enticing them to switch from Brand A to Brand B is only suited to consumers who already know they need a specific type of product, who are willing to try Brand B for the sake of comparison, but who know they can always swap back to Brand A on their next purchase if they want to. This is suited to consumer goods, not corporate purchasing where swapping brands involves a supply contract that can last years, where multiple stakeholders who influence procurement decisions must be won over through months of relationship building, and where not every executive may believe a problem exists that they need to act on.

You can test whether your company's sales and marketing is designed for retail consumers or for B2B buyers by asking the people who do your marketing to answer three questions:

1. What is the business challenge our target customers have?
2. How does this manifest as a problem at the executive level?
3. Which messages most effectively drive executives to explore solutions to this problem?

It doesn't take long to see if a disconnect exists. If marketers can answer questions 1–3 cogently, it's a good sign that they understand the B2B marketing strategy you need to underpin your e-mail marketing. But if they have no clue, chances are the marketing they're using to create leads for you is based on transactional retail marketing, not strategic solution marketing. If your volume or quality of lead generation has been weak, this might be a reason.

DON'T COMMUNICATE VALUE, CREATE IT

In an interview with SalesLobby.com, Neil Rackham (author of *SPIN Selling* and coauthor of *Rethinking the Sales Force*) commented on the effect the Internet had on traditional selling models, and suggested what lay in store:

> Information-based selling, the talking brochure selling, is just going to die out because you can't afford it when it's more costly and less convenient; and until the Internet came along you had to have it because you had no alternative. We think of the Internet sometimes as a selling medium, but in fact it's a buying medium. Most business-to-business commerce on the Internet is initiated by the buyer, not the seller. Salespeople of the future have to actually create value, not communicate value. We've done surveys where we've asked customers, have you ever had a salesperson call on you where you would have written them a personal check for [the value of the] sales call? To those that said yes, we said, tell us about it. The most common single factor in what they described is that this salesperson *"changed the way I thought about my problems. I did something very differently as a result of talking to them."* Now, if you're going to do that with your customers, you've got to be much more challenging, you've got to be able to come in as business equals, you've got to focus on the problem and not on the product.[7]

We suggest that this process starts with the e-mails you send out and the landing pages you link them to. A best practice is to focus on what's called the *buyer's journey*, a term coined by Hugh Macfarlane in his book *The Leaky Funnel*. Understanding the triggers that cause a buyer to start looking for a solution, then playing a part in stimulating or creating awareness of these drivers, is the essence of creating demand (this is what we traditionally call "marketing"). Then the next task is to create value in a way that satisfies the buyer's emotional and logical needs, at a pace that matches the cadence of their buying process, and ask for the decision at the appropriate time (this is what we traditionally call "sales").

As stated earlier, if you're getting lackluster results from your current lead creation, use e-mail, social selling, and other technologies to take control of flow and quality yourself.

Let's look at some of the essentials . . .

E-mail Marketing

A 2017 Smart Insights report[8] of cross-industry statistics from MailChimp, Silverpop (now part of IBM), and GetResponse reveals the effectiveness of e-mail marketing campaigns. Before looking at the statistics, let's get clear on some e-mail marketing terminology.

Open Rate (OR) is defined as the percentage of e-mails that reaches an in-box and are not bounced or returned as "undeliverable."

Click-to-Open Rate (CTOR) indicates how many recipients saw the e-mail then clicked to read it, compared with ignoring or deleting it.

Click-Through Rate (CTR) tells you how many recipients reading an e-mail went on to click a link inside that e-mail.

The first insight from the data is that nearly two-thirds of all e-mails are now opened on mobile devices. If your prospecting e-mails don't have copy and creative designed to be read, swiped, and tapped on tablet and smartphone screens, you're designing them for an extinct buyer.

Straightforward text works fine. But if you're adding copy, creative artwork, and graphics, make it mobile-friendly or risk deletion. Cut paragraphs to bullet points. Use infographics.

Once your e-mail is sent, you hope it will reach the intended recipients and enjoy a high Open Rate. If your OR is low and the bounce rate is high, it can mean you have a lot of nonexistent e-mail addresses, mailboxes are full, or the e-mail campaign is regarded as spam and rejected by servers. There are whole books and blogs on how to avoid e-mail bouncing and blacklisting.

OPEN RATE BY INDUSTRY	PERCENT
Automobiles and transportation	27.3
Banks and financial services	23.3
Computer hardware and telecommunications	24.9
Computer software and online services	20.8
Consumer products	25.1
Consumer services	21.6
Corporate services	23.0
Floor service, sports, and entertainment	20.7
Hospitals, healthcare, and biotech	26.1
Industrial manufacturing and utilities	25.9
Insurance	27.5
Lodging, travel agencies, and services	22.7
Marketing agencies and services	18.2
Media and publishing	19.3
Nonprofits, associations, and government	26.4
Real estate, construction, and building products	25.6
Retail and e-commerce	20.5
Schools and education	30.9

Figure 2.4 E-mail Open Rate by Industry, 2017

A benchmark of e-mails sent by 750 large enterprise executives in 40 countries reveals which industries gain the highest Open Rate percentages (Figure 2.4).

For example, if you mount an e-mail campaign to banking and financial services clients, you can expect an Open Rate of 23.3 percent. If you have 10,000 names on an e-mail list, then 2,320 will reach the intended in-box.

The next success you want is the "Click to Open Rate." In Figure 2.5, we see prospects in banking and financial services have a CTOR of 12.0 percent. This means out of the 2,320 e-mails that

CLICK TO OPEN RATE BY INDUSTRY	PERCENT
Automobiles and transportation	11.0
Banks and financial services	12.0
Computer hardware and telecommunications	16.2
Computer software and online services	10.1
Consumer products	12.9
Consumer services	14.0
Corporate services	12.5
Floor service, sports, and entertainment	13.6
Hospitals, healthcare, and biotech	12.2
Industrial manufacturing and utilities	11.7
Insurance	11.4
Lodging, travel agencies, and services	9.2
Marketing agencies and services	10.7
Media and publishing	12.9
Nonprofits, associations, and government	19.4
Real estate, construction, and building products	13.1
Retail and e-commerce	15.0
Schools and education	11.2

Figure 2.5 CTOR by Industry, 2017

reached their in-boxes, 280 will be clicked on. From this data, we don't know if the executive you targeted is the actual viewer, or if their assistant is serving as a human filter, but your message has been seen by somebody looking at the executive's e-mail account.

You can keep track of whether you're achieving a CTOR on par with your industry peers by searching online for "e-mail marketing benchmarks." Various companies like Smart Insights, Campaign Monitor, and MailChimp publish annual statistics by industry which is worth comparing your efforts against.

So, in our fictional campaign to banks and financial services executives, we now have 280 views. Out of the 10,000 names we launched to, there is a hit rate of 2.8 percent.

What happens next? Ideally you want the executive (or their assistant) to react to something they see and click a link. It's this all-important Click-Through Rate (CTR) that indicates interest. In most countries, this click qualifies as a sign of interest that provides legal permission to e-mail that person again and have it not be regarded as spam.

In the paper "The State of Email Marketing By Industry," Kath Pay of GetResponse[9] shows that banks and financial services have a CTR of 2.99 percent. This means that of our 280 views, 8 people will click the e-mail in response to something they see and visit the website or campaign page you point them to. The net effect of this is that, after sending out 10,000 e-mails, 8 people will click to know more on a first contact in that industry. This is an end-to-end response rate of 0.08 percent—a little less than one-tenth of one percent.

This may look like a depressingly low response rate. But don't fret. CTOR and CTR trend higher when it's not the first time the executive has been exposed to your brand; or if you're targeting them after they showed interest at a trade show, conference, or webinar; or if they're a happy current or past customer you're attempting to cross-sell; or if they're an unhappy customer of your competitor looking to make a change; and when your e-mail design is clean, the copy is compelling, and there's a clear call to action. All these factors increase responsiveness and are explored in more detail later in this chapter.

Cadence

First, a word about cadence. This is where you make decisions about the right time to kick off an e-mail campaign, the right number of unique messages to send out (using content the executive will value), and how often the executive should receive these e-mails from you. Too few makes you forgettable; too many makes you a pest.

A rule of thumb is to send e-mails out 25 percent more frequently than you think the customer can stand. If you're nervous about over-e-mailing an executive prospect for fear they will unsubscribe and opt out, you risk under-e-mailing them—which limits their ability to engage with you. The reality is that if your content is good quality, they won't unsubscribe. Sure, they might only glance at it, but drip by drip your brand will start to be recognized as one that talks about issues that add value until the time comes that the executive is aware that they have a problem or need and are ready to engage.

You can't control that. All you can do is keep your brand in front of them and write messages designed to educate them on problems they should be dealing with or give new insight into a relevant business area. You must resist the urge to talk about your product at this stage! Eventually there will come a click to know more, but you can't force it.

Anyone who unsubscribes because they're receiving too much good content from you is not a target customer. Let your competitors win these.

The goal is to send your e-mail marketing to executives aggressively to start with, then taper off in frequency. A recommended sequence for an outbound campaign is to send a new unique e-mail on Days 1, 4, 8, 15, and 25 of the month, then repeat the following month. This drip-feed approach leads to compounding returns over time as your brand becomes familiar, your content gets recognized, and one day your headline, copy, or graphic makes a connection that causes the executive to click through to know more.

E-mail Campaign Pages

Research compiled by Kissmetrics[10] reveals that an e-mail campaign landing page or even your main corporate website has a maximum of 10 seconds to make an impression. This statistic is validated in a separate study from Microsoft Research that analyzed page-visit durations on nearly 206,000 web pages by more than 10,000 visitors [more than 2 billion (2,000,000,000) unique visits].[11] They found the probability of a prospect leaving your website is highest during the first few seconds because their past experience with poorly designed websites has made them harsh critics, so they perform a ruthless triage and abandon weak websites quickly, as can be seen in Figure 2.6 from Nielsen Norman Group.

It's rare for people to linger, but when a page survives the all-important 10-second barrier, users will stay and look around a while, though they're still likely to leave in the next 20 seconds unless something meaningful catches their eye. Only after they've stayed on your page for 30 seconds does attrition flatten out. After this, visitors will keep leaving every second, but at a slower rate.

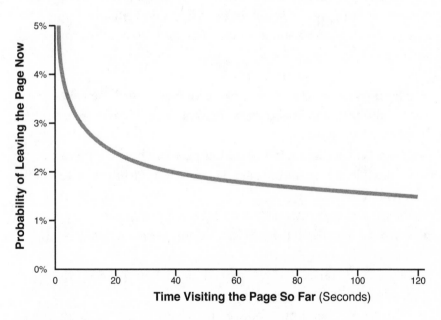

Figure 2.6 Likelihood of a Visitor Leaving Your Web Page

If you can convince your prospects to stay on your page for half a minute, they'll usually stay for two minutes—but rarely longer. The bottom line here is that a weak web page will lose people within seconds. The best web pages might keep them for a couple of minutes at best.

Whatever you want them to read or do while on your page, make it readable or doable within this time limit. Does knowing this make you want to rethink how your campaign landing pages are designed? E-mail marketing should lead people to simple sites, with relevant headlines, easily read text, and a rapid call to action— especially when viewed on mobile devices. This is why single-page scrolling sites became popular, and why companies stopped pointing e-mail links to their corporate website (often an encyclopedic repository of information about the business) and instead created e-mail campaign-specific minisites or landing pages designed for the express purpose of satisfying the 10-second rule.

Kissmetrics offers some well-researched tips to improve page impact[12]:

- Having a prominent value proposition as a headline is key.
- Headlines that describe your customer's problem increase retention by 31 percent.
- A clear call to action increases engagement by 105.9 percent.
- Red call to action buttons are 34 percent more effective than buttons in other colors.
- Videos increase interest by 144 percent.
- If you want prospects to fill in a sign-up form, make it less than 5 fields.
- Using "Get started today" instead of "See our pricing" increases action by 252 percent.
- Adding a "chat now" button increases response rates by 31 percent.

- The inclusion of social proof (i.e., testimonials) improves stickiness by 144 percent.
- Photos of people and faces are better than photos of products.

Pop-up Windows, Chats, and Response Times

Ethan Denney, cofounder of ConvertFlow, comments on the value of pop-up windows on web pages you design as destinations for your marketing e-mails: "You've probably been engaged by some sort of pop-up device. If these are well-timed, and offer something of value, you take action if you see the offer as helpful. These can be triggered a number of seconds after a visitor lands on a page, after scrolling a certain percentage of the page, when clicking a certain button/link, or when exiting a webpage."[13] Justin Rondeau at Econsultancy agrees: "A site with an overlay garners up to 400% more email opt-ins than a site that relies on an in-line form."[14] This is an astonishing statistic.

You can improve lead conversion even more when you connect to an executive in real time as they visit your website or campaign landing page. Dr. James Oldroyd at the Kellogg School of Management notes, "71% of Internet leads are lost because companies don't respond fast enough."[15] Popular methods to make contact are via a chat window, e-mail, or phone call (if you collected their contact data already). The idea is to do so before their interest fades and your brand recognition is replaced by something else that catches their eye.

You are 100 times less likely to make contact with a prospect if your first follow-up is more than 30 minutes after they submit an online form, and 500 times less likely if you wait more than 5 hours.[16] Ideally, you will put in place a system that automatically triggers an alert when a visitor clicks the link in your e-mail and lands on a predefined page. It's a proven fact that executives are most likely to engage further during and immediately after they've first interacted with your online content.

Due to the rapid pace of business today, the level of competition, and executive buyers' increasing acceptance of technology, older marketing tactics about teasing a prospect through several gateways as you qualify them before making contact are being replaced by a return to the old adage "strike while the iron is hot." You can't afford to let a prospect go cold.

One company that does this impressively well is IWG plc, formerly Regus, a provider of virtual office and serviced office packages. At the time of writing, an e-mail campaign hit us from IWG. Coincidentally we were nearing the end of the lease for one of our offices and were considering moving to a virtual model. We clicked the e-mail and were led to a page overlaid with a pop-up window that immediately asked if we wanted a callback in exchange for our name and phone number. Like most prospects newly arrived at an unfamiliar site, we closed the pop-up without filling it in, and took a self-guided tour.

The site led us expertly. It had clear headlines. Copy (all the text) was brief and kept us engaged. Images were contextually relevant, showing lots of smiling faces of people using each service. It took less than a minute to find a serviced office option that appealed, with a bright red button for "Get a quote." We clicked this expecting to see a price list, but IWG didn't give its pricing data for free. They knew we needed pricing as a next step, so withheld it unless we traded our contact information, which we did. Clicking a red "Send me my quote" button saw an e-mail arrive within 15 seconds with pricing attached. This was impressive.

Even more impressive was the phone ringing within two minutes, as we were engaged by a local salesperson who asked smart questions, knew their product, and were pleasant yet assertive in their goal to "help us make the move to a virtual office." The words and tone they used conveyed that they saw their role as a facilitator who could help us complete a journey we had already started. They didn't sound at all like a salesperson trying to close a sale to pocket the commission. Yes, we signed up. It was a textbook example of e-mail marketing done well.

Clearly the type of service IWG offers is for the mass market and transactional. It can be promoted by e-mail then end in a sale within minutes. Your product or service may be more complex than this and require multiple meetings with several people over weeks or months before a contract can be agreed. In the long game of solution selling, e-mail marketing's best utility may be as a support tool to build your brand recognition as a credible player in your industry, as a provider of relevant, quality content, and as a way to test an executive's temperature by offering regular calls to action until they bite.

While doing this, don't forget the power of going Old School and asking your network for introductions and referrals, sending prospecting letters by snail mail (so rare today they actually stand out), posting magazine articles with handwritten sticky notes explaining why certain passages are relevant to their business—anything to show you're a player on the same stage and have their best interests in mind. Don't give up quickly. Be consistent. Persistence pays off.

Now that we've explored how to get noticed, the next part of the puzzle is to learn the latest approaches for gaining access to executives and creating value at the C-Suite. That discussion starts in the next chapter.

CHAPTER SUMMARY

Let's summarize what we've discussed in this chapter by looking at the three key messages:

1. *Executives with an active need have already checked you out on the Internet.* When executives recognize a need, they start their own research by talking to people whose opinions they value and by doing their own detective work on the Internet. If they use a search engine to research the problem they have, they probably won't find most of the companies addressing it, because most companies' websites use sales language (product), not buying language (problem). If they find the right product categories to look at, executives will quickly become expert enough on your company and your competitors to eliminate the need to meet with you for information. They will usually set the vision for a project and then delegate the management of vendors to someone at a lower level.

2. *Executives with a latent need aren't looking for you . . . yet.* Roughly two-thirds of a target market may be unaware that alternatives to the way they do business today exist. They remain untroubled by current or impending problems because those problems are simply not front-of-mind. If you help an executive see that she has a problem and she becomes troubled by it, you are on the scene at the origin of her thought process, and that involvement implies that you may have the answers she needs. More than half the sales opportunities where demand is created in this way do not go to competitive tender. Of those that do go to tender, more than half are won by the first company to engage the executive on these issues, even if the executive delegates vendor management to lower levels of the organization.

3. *Take responsibility for your own prospecting and lead generation.* Don't rely solely on your marketing team to find new leads. Technology like LinkedIn and Viadeo allows you to prowl a social network of potential buyers, see their connections, and gain exposure via blogs and referrals. E-mail apps like MailChimp and Capterra can broadcast responsive e-mail campaigns that you can control on the go from a smartphone. Social apps like Twitter, WhatsApp, and Pinterest give further traction, and you can manage all your social media in one location through Hootsuite, Buffer, or Sprout Social. You can then track success in your chosen CRM, from ACT! to Salesforce. The tools are here, they're affordable, and they give you personal control over the inputs that drive your outputs. No self-respecting salesperson should ever place their earning potential in the hands of another. So get the right apps, pick up the phone on a regular basis, and hit the bricks to expand your network every week. It's also worth staying up to date on advances in machine learning and artificial intelligence as they make lead management more precise and automated.

Chapter 3

Understanding What Executives Want

Understanding what motivates senior executives requires a keen understanding of their company's key business issues, including the business drivers that are creating the need for change and the initiatives the company has put in place to address those drivers. These issues may have a different impact on each senior executive in the client organization—mostly depending on the executive's specific function and role. In some cases, this information is easy to obtain (by reading the President's Letter in a recent annual report, for example), but in other cases, it may require a substantial amount of digging.

In any case, executives expect salespeople to be prepared and have a basic knowledge of the key issues facing them—before you meet them. They don't want to educate you on information that can be readily obtained, either from a public source like the Internet or from lower-level executives in the organization, whom they presume you already worked with before reaching the C-Suite.

Start by being aware of your client's internal and external business drivers. Any of these can create a need for change and be deemed important enough to assign people, money, and time to. These drivers are where sales opportunities are first forged. You learn most about how these pressures affect the customer by talking to them, but you should do your own research on them first to get an idea about what winds of change are sweeping your client's industry, and what terminology is current and topical. This helps you talk like an insider. It also helps you put into context how your products and services might allow the company to perform a task or achieve an outcome better, faster, easier, or with less risk, which is the only reason an executive will mandate a change from their current supplier or the status quo. This chapter focuses on explanations from executives about why it is important for salespeople to understand what drives them.

HOW TO DO HIGHLY EFFECTIVE RESEARCH

Doing the legwork to fully understand an executive's needs is the foundation for evolving into a Trusted Advisor salesperson, yet many salespeople we work with confess it's a challenge to find time to read industry magazines or business periodicals, or profile the client's current affairs on the Internet, or get along to symposiums and conferences to learn the client's issues and jargon. If you aspire to create value for the C-Suite, be a Trusted Advisor, and engage executives early in the buying cycle, this is your price for admission. There are no short cuts. Immerse yourself in your prospect's world.

Look at the faces to the left and right of you at your next sales team meeting, or the names that appear on the register of your next conference call. A majority of people you work with don't do this and never have. It's a habit only the very elite practice. The knowledge they collect helps them rise above the herd of regular salespeople, getting recognized as industry specialists and business peers to executives who don't have time to spend with reps who simply pitch a project, but readily draw into their inner circle people who sound like they belong on the board, talk their language, challenge conventional thinking, and offer upsides.

A few hours a week is all it takes to brush up on the latest events across industries. If you don't make the time to do research, information won't pop into your head by itself.

Top salespeople we have met around the world always do four things to "go to school" on their customers and avoid becoming irrelevant.

1. Get in the Game

Economies boom and bust in roughly 10-year cycles. When it's a bull market, it's business as usual. But when it's a bear market, buyers tighten their belts and sharpen their pencils. A great many executives are told the only reasonable reflex in a downturn is to adopt a scarcity mentality and slash spending. Their company's financial and risk managers anticipate supply chain interruptions, rising interest rates, volatility in import costs, contract cancellations, and payment defaults. To get ahead of these risks they suggest to their bosses that the company should freeze new staff hires, postpone new initiatives, prune the existing workforce, liquidate inventory to release cash, drop prices, and cut all but essential operational and capital expenditure.

Executives told us they all have different levels of risk tolerance, but when a sensible business idea is presented to them, they're prepared to listen and consider it. They keep their heads when everyone else is shedding staff, canceling ad space, trimming R&D budgets, and taking their foot off the gas. They see others cutting back as an opportunity to pick up the industry's best talent, get the next generation of products ready to leapfrog competitors when the rebound comes, and keep their brand prominent so when buyers start spending again, theirs is the brand that maintained mindshare. They spend prudently, but don't stop altogether.

Top sellers function accordingly. They figure out ways to help executives take advantage of opportunity. They know selling is not a spectator sport and don't wait to be invited to the table, but rather get into the game of being rainmakers. They believe: "I can maximize my value to my customer executives this year by learning all I can about them, their company, their competitors, and their industry, and bringing them new ideas they can then pay me to implement. The more I mean to them, the more they will mean to me."

What we're saying here is that to get in the game is to take the initiative, to be a change agent, to be curious enough to ask, "Why not?" and "What if?" about your customer's business, and get ideas out to them. Can you immediately get an audience with every executive and make them listen? No. But there's nothing stopping you posting an article on LinkedIn about the issues you see in an industry and making a case for change there.

Blog a different topic each week. Explore different facets of the problems you know customers in your market are facing. Propose ways the problems can be solved. Cite case studies of where you've done it before. Take your smartphone along to friendly customers and get their permission to film them talking about your solutions in action, and post these in your blogs, on the business Facebook page you run alongside your personal Facebook page, or on that business-focused YouTube or Vimeo channel you run.

Yes, you should be doing all of this. Top sellers build their own brand and do their own marketing. Why? Because they're in the game. They don't rely wholly on their company's marketing department any more than they plan to share their commissions with them. Top sellers make it rain. They take personal responsibility for hitting and then overachieving their sales quota. Why? Because they're in the game.

You may not get immediate results. After people receive your posts six or more times, you'll start to make a dent. People will see you. Your network will comment on your posts and share them with others. Now you're in syndication. You'll be tempted to reply to comments as they come in. Don't. The idea is to let the initial fire burn a few days, and when the comments and reposts start to thin out, *then* reply to one person's comment. The fact that someone else's LinkedIn account has been updated by your comment brings it to the attention of the people in *their* network. When they click to see the update on their friend, they see your post, and *they* might share it with others who will also comment. And so the cycle starts again. This is how you keep fanning the flame. You can breathe life into one blog or post for months using this method, and it's how you lift your viewer count from several close friends to thousands of strangers, some of whom will be potential customers. When they see enough good content and value from you, they start to subscribe to you. Now you're making a difference. People follow you.

Yes, now you're in the game.

2. Work Backward

This is where you visualize where an executive might want to be. Start with the end in mind, then plan backwards, thinking of the things they must put in place to make that vision a reality. To do this you must use your research to see where the executive wants to take their company or department next, or you must take an educated guess based on what you've seen others do. It helps to form an opinion on why they're not achieving their vision and what's been holding them back. Is it because they don't know there's a better way? Do they lack the appetite to change, the manpower, the resources or capital? Your job is to offer a way to fill in these gaps.

Map out ministeps they can take to get from their current state to the future state, identify the pros versus the cons, the risks versus the benefits, the costs versus the savings or profit of each step, and the time needed to complete them. This type of backwards planning is something people in the executive's company can't do. Why? Because they're an expert in how the problem manifests, they're not an expert in solving it. If they were, the problem would already be dealt with. The fact that it isn't solved already, yet remains visible means they're in need, and where there's a need there's an opportunity.

You're the expert in solving this problem. You're the experienced navigator who can steer them through the change process. After all, you do this every day, don't you? This is your domain. Own it. Be bold. Take charge. Executives tell us it frustrates them when salespeople do everything right to earn a place at the table, then act like they expect the executive to know what they want and issue instructions. This is a reactive, order-taker mentality, and executives get enough of that from their own subordinates. You got in the game and created a road map from a possible future state to the current state. Step up and show some thought leadership. Executives love it when salespeople take charge. Your confidence fills them with confidence.

3. Adopt a Routine

One of the behaviors observed in Gen X and Y workers (now in senior sales and management roles) and Gen Z workers (now entering the sales profession) is that being raised in an era of *instant everything*, they can eschew activities where results are not immediate. This makes research a casualty because it requires patience and doesn't have a fast payoff. Similarly, some old sales dogs who have worked the same territory for years may feel they know everything that's going on by osmosis. Both are mistaken.

To connect to the issues that matter to executives, research is not an activity you can do now and then. It's a matter of personal accountability to being a professional. If you don't schedule a *sacrosanct* time each week to sit down and study your customers, nobody else will step in and do it for you. Except maybe your competitors.

Make it a habit. Schedule it in your calendar and protect that appointment as though it were your most important customer meeting. Naturally it needs to be outside your prime selling hours when customers are most responsive to calls, and around internal meetings you can't avoid. With Tuesdays to Thursdays being the best days to reach executives, and 8 a.m. to 2 p.m. being when energy and attention for a business discussion is at its highest,[1] you don't want to use these times to do research. You should be selling at those times. Instead, schedule your research on Mondays or Fridays. As stated earlier, protect this appointment. You'll be tempted to use the time if there's a chance of seeing a customer who's been hard to nail down. Only you can gauge if it's worth making an exception. Just know that when you start to get casual with research and drop it from your regular routine, it's very easy to never get back into the habit. Top sellers don't let that happen, and executives wish it didn't either, because the better educated you are on their world, the more you can do for them and the more work they'll award you.

4. Ask Lots of Questions

We once heard an area sales manager coach their team as follows: "An executive is someone who has no time to listen to you, but all day to talk to you." It can be lonely at the top, and that creates a paradox. The very people you might expect an executive to be most open with (for example, their peer officers and subordinates) are the ones they may confide in the least. A leader with doubts about their staff or concerns about their company's future may not tell those people, and certainly not the press or analysts. They have an image to maintain. But they may open up to a salesperson who has established rapport and trust with them, whose questions reveal an intimacy with those specific problems and concerns.

But let's remember the wisdom of all lawyers: "Never ask a question without knowing where the answer might lead." This is why research is important. When you study your customers' businesses, you learn their issues—and can have an opinion ready on the various implications and choices available to deal with those issues. This foreknowledge allows you to ask questions with confidence, because you're already equipped to follow the conversation into any rabbit hole it might go down, and still sound credible. It's through smart questions that you steer the conversation and keep control.

Controlling the conversation with questions doesn't mean you rein it in to match a predetermined script. You must allow an executive the freedom to go on tangents and follow trains of thought as a result of your questions, because this is where their personal attitudes, impressions, and ideas get revealed. You use questions like a rudder, to steer them to an appropriate outcome for the meeting.

THE VALUE OF RESEARCH

As an aid to researching your customers, a step-by-step "Guide to Client Discovery" is provided in Appendix A of this book. This has already been road tested by thousands of salespeople who graduated from our workshops and offers practical advice on using the Internet and other resources to stay abreast of customer developments.

Gaining a deep understanding of an executive's issues, pressures, and drivers helps you anticipate their future requirements and better see how the products and services you provide are relevant. Competitive salespeople use this information in discussions to explore potential needs and signal that they can add business value. Demystifying the C-Suite is all about doing your homework.

Here's what one sales professional shared on this topic:

Senior-level executives are very busy, and they want some assurance that meeting with you is worth their time. It's like a job interview. A candidate needs to show relevant experience on their CV or résumé and come to the interview able to talk about the issues that are important to the employer. You can't know what those issues are unless you do your homework. For salespeople, every sales call is a job interview—we're serial job hunters! When I'm preparing for an executive sales call, I try to determine the specific business value I might put on the table. I look at the customer's website and google phrases like "strategy" and "press release" connected to the company, plus the names of the top executives associated with the company's competitors. Sometimes I'll add the names of the company's biggest customers to see what they're doing in the market and if my prospect is (or should be) proactive about serving those needs. I also refine those searches to show only the past three to six months so that what I read is current. It's amazing how many investor presentations, analyst reports, or journalist reviews you can find. This tells me the customer's language, their strategy, and what their rivals are doing. This type of research might take an hour or two, but that's the discipline you need to be ready for the hour in front of the executive. So when my competitors meet the same executive and ask, "What are your top three business objectives?" I can be in there saying, "I understand your top three business objectives are X, Y, and Z; which one is most important to you and why?" You see the difference? I'm able to show that I did my homework and earn the right to ask for something the Internet can't give me—the executive's insight! These are the discussions that make sales, and why doing your homework is the best preparation for demystifying the C-Suite.

We're big fans of this type of preparation. But having run thousands of sales coaching sessions over the years, we're still amazed at how many salespeople fail to do it.

Case in point: an invitation came in to help a sales team review its plan for a million-dollar deal at a new prospect they'd been trying to land for a couple of years. The team sold customer analytics software. The prospect was a leading cable TV brand. The opportunity plan explained they "wanted to segment their customers better."

We gave that opportunity plan a forensic examination and quickly saw that the team members enjoyed strong mentor relationships with two midlevel managers in the department where the product would be installed. But despite knowing these people, the sales team wasn't learning enough about them, wasn't networking to other people likely to impact the decision, and hadn't lifted the conversation above the technical features of their product. They were painting themselves as a transactional Commodity Supplier, not a Trusted Advisor.

Before our coaching call, we invested two hours on Google to collect our own intelligence on the prospect. We learned they had recently shuffled their executive managers around. We wrote this down. We did background searches on each of these people and found some of them had presented papers at recent conferences and been cited in magazines talking about issues important to them. We wrote this down. Then we searched for links between these people and the sales team's rivals and found recent competitor press releases that cited sales made into that company and which customer executives made the decisions to buy. We wrote down what we found.

We learned the CIO had inherited his job from one of the company's original founders, who had signed a multimillion-dollar deal three years earlier with the main competitor of the team we were coaching. Would the newly appointed CIO reverse a decision made by a member of the family that owned the company? Not without a compelling reason.

Unless this sales team could find a way to meet other executives of high rank and influence and build support with them, they would be facing a brick wall.

A few more clicks and we read that the prospect had recently raised billions of dollars to buy the company's shares back from investors and delist it from the stock market. They wanted to return to private company status so they could invest in infrastructure without their spending being blocked by shareholders. We wrote this down. In the past six months this prospect had acquired a major newspaper, was funding the rollout of broadband Wi-Fi across several large cities, and was adding new HD channels to its regional cable and satellite packages. We wrote this down.

The board was clearly transforming the company into a media powerhouse, cross-pollinating online and print entertainment, information, and advertising. To do that effectively, it would need to promote the right packages to the right customers at the right time through the right marketing channel—the sort of capability you get from great customer analytics software.

When we dialed into the sales team coaching call, we opened with questions like: "Why does the database marketing team need your product?" and "Is anything happening at a business level that might be driving this at the technical level?" The members of the sales team talked about the technical brief and how they were the perfect fit, but didn't see the bigger picture. After we shared what we had uncovered, there was stunned silence, then a murmur of hope. Half an hour later, the team members had created a new plan of attack and understood what this prospect was really trying to achieve. And at last, *they* wrote it down.

With a little bit of effort, they now saw the context of the sale and were better prepared to add value to the thought process of the executives they were already talking with, and others they would go on to meet. Several months later they won a multimillion-dollar supply contract, despite a competitor having the advantage as an incumbent supplier, and a prior relationship with a company founder.

This is why good customer profiling can be a game changer. Salespeople ignore doing it at their peril. This is confirmed by research that indicates a significant difference in results between those who do customer research to ask informed questions and have cogent business discussions, and those who don't put in this groundwork.

Dialogue Review published the findings of researchers who spent two years analyzing more than a million minutes of telephone and face-to-face conversations between salespeople and executive customers in the United States, Canada, England, Scotland, Wales,

France, and Germany,[2] which were recorded with the customer's consent. These audio tracks were run through speech analytics software to isolate the voiceprints and track the sequence in which typical selling and buying phrases were heard. Each phrase was mapped to a list of sales competencies, and this served to unlock a picture of which skills are used most often, and in which sequence by each type of sales role. The commercial outcome of each sale was then captured over a two-year period.

Some calls went nowhere. A few closed in a single meeting. Others didn't produce an immediate sale, but progressed to a further meeting over subsequent weeks or months. From this the researchers were able to follow specific sales opportunities from start to end and see which skills were most relevant for each stage of sale. They were also able to isolate examples of each skill being executed poorly or at the wrong time compared to being executed properly. The resulting sales revenue was also logged to see which skill combinations made the biggest financial impact, and how often each type of skill was used by reps who went on to be high, middle, or low performers.

Relevant to this chapter, only 24 percent of salespeople were heard referring to the executive's business drivers early in the sale. Of these, only one-third (8 percent of all salespeople) brought these points up again when explaining their value proposition. It was recorded that salespeople who did so heard 76 percent fewer objections, faced 61 percent fewer discount requests, and closed their sales more or less on the forecast date, compared to the other 92 percent of salespeople. All of the salespeople who did their homework and used it throughout the sale went on to achieve their annual target.

Of course, there's more to winning a sale than researching your customer. But we see a clear correlation between those who do so and the level of credibility, control, and success they enjoy.

THE DRIVERS OF EXECUTIVE DECISION MAKING

Figure 3.1 depicts the drivers that are most likely to be behind your customer's thought process when it comes to making investments with suppliers.

Think of the image as a cross section of an arm. It shows the white "bone" in the center, surrounded by the "muscles" in gray. In this visual analogy, we'll say the bone represents internal factors that provide stability to a company, typified by operational and financial resources such as money, talent, infrastructure, procedures, culture, systems, and measurement, all of which are used to underpin performance.

The company's bones are connected to the outside world through muscles that affect and in turn are affected by six different external factors: the supply chain drivers of *suppliers, business partners,* and *customers,* and the marketplace drivers of *competitors, globalization,* and *regulatory issues* (we've included a business issues worksheet to help you profile these drivers in Appendix B of this book).

Let's examine what each of the eight drivers means to you as a salesperson.

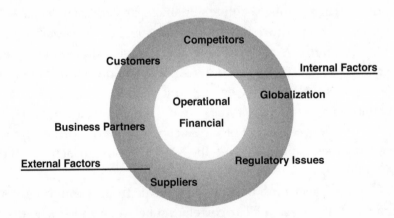

Figure 3.1 Drivers of Executive Decision Making

Financial Drivers

Every executive is under financial pressure to perform. At the most basic level, executives must do one of two things to produce a profit: increase revenue or reduce costs. For salespeople to build business value for an executive who is pressured by financial drivers, they must ultimately help the executive move the needle on either profit or cost, and do so in a way that's consistent with how their industry measures success. Each industry will use different jargon that relates to how they measure their business and its financial performance.

For example, in the airline industry, drivers such as load factor, a variable planning horizon, high seasonality, fierce competition, excessive government intervention, high fixed costs, and low margins (while the airline industry generates billions of dollars, it has a cumulative profit margin of less than 1 percent)[3] are relevant financial drivers you should be conversant with. Show how your solution improves these and you'll get the executive's attention.

If you're selling to a bank, different drivers are of interest. For example: customer loyalty, share of wallet, reducing fraud and unrecoverable debts, consolidating and upgrading infrastructure, transparency, legislative compliance, merchant alliances, and so on.

The jargon a company uses to talk about its business is like a tribal language. As a rule, it's unwise to throw those labels around hoping to make an impression unless you truly understand their interpretations and implications. To cite an old Spanish proverb: "It is better to stay silent and conceal one's knowledge than to speak and reveal one's ignorance."

Today it takes no time at all to google an unfamiliar phrase or search for "top issues affecting X industry" to get educated. And if you encounter something you never heard before while in discussion, don't fake an understanding lest you be tested on it. Simply say, "To be sure I understand that topic the way you do, could you explain what you mean in a bit more detail?" Executives appreciate honesty, and don't mind clarifying as long as they're not teaching you from scratch.

Operational Drivers

Executives concern themselves with trying to determine how to improve the internal organization and affect the financial return based on that improvement. At the most basic level, executives are concerned with having the right strategy, taking advantage of the latest approaches, and having the right people, processes, and technologies to execute that strategy.

One executive in our study looks to salespeople as gateways for "expertise we don't have, coupled with experience for producing this type of capability."

Look at how you can help executives do a better job of making, quality controlling, selling, and delivering their business plan. All of these will be affected by the effectiveness (doing the right things) and efficiencies (doing things right) in the operation.

Supplier Drivers

As a result of Six Sigma, Total Quality Management, and Supply Chain Reengineering, large companies are routinely reducing the number of suppliers they buy materials and services from in the hope that buying more from a smaller pool of suppliers creates less complexity, simpler accounting, and improved buying power.

If you are an executive in a company that is on the *selling side* of the supply chain, your first concern is about winning the contract, then about preserving quality and margins with buyers who know how important their trade is to you and will try to reduce your price at every contract renewal. If you aggregate parts of your offering from different locations, you will obsess over the smallest fluctuations in foreign exchange rates, gasoline prices, labor costs, political policy, and even how changes in the weather might interrupt your just-in-time manufacturing and supply logistics. Buying too much raw material, having too many pallets aging in warehouses and on wharves, or losing too many crates in transit equates to poor Supply Chain Management. Finding the right balance is something you want to achieve.

If you are an executive on the *buying side* of the supply chain, your concern is with the reliability of supply, quality, economies of scale, inventory turnover, shrinkage through loss or theft, warehousing and distribution technologies, demand forecasting, and many of the same issues that trouble executives on the selling side of the supply chain. There's very much a level of interdependence between the buyer and the seller, so approaches to real-time data sharing, shared infrastructure, and shared risk management remain compelling issues to discuss, especially when a salesperson can cogently explain how any of his company's solutions in these areas can do the job faster, better, or with less risk than the way the executive does it today.

Business Partner Drivers

At times, new alliances are created between former competitors in order to thwart a competitor they share in common, as advised by the Arabian proverb: "The enemy of my enemy is my friend." Your customers may even now be evaluating their business partner relationships in light of changing business environments. This represents another opportunity to create value by demonstrating an understanding of the customer's pressures and offering solutions by orchestrating relevant introductions to your company's network of people, partners, and affiliates who have value to add. Solutions are sometimes more about the relationships you help broker than about the product or service you sell.

If you were the executive you're selling to, your thoughts might regularly turn to pondering how to find new business partners, ensuring that they are the right fit, keeping them informed and educated, testing the quality of what they do and its effect on your brand, avoiding channel conflict, and making the relationship profitable. So put yourself in the executive's shoes. Explore how she does these things today, and you may see ways in which your company can make a positive difference. The executive will listen.

Customer Drivers

Maintaining and growing their existing customer base, creating and enhancing loyalty, and delivering value are of prime importance to most executives. But how do you target the right customers? How do you anticipate their needs? How do you develop new products that will be ready when the market starts to demand them? How can you tell which customers are your best ones? How can you keep your best customers loyal? How do you balance your business so that it's not overly dependent on a small list of customers who do most of the spending? As a salesperson, if you can demonstrate how your product or service can add value in these areas, you will be seen as a resource who can help create a competitive advantage, and executives will want to talk to you if they recognize that they have a problem in this area.

According to one account manager who sells to the financial services industry:

> You have to first understand the client's business and the demands on that business. We talk about the company's unique situations. For example, some brokerage houses have investment tools that are out of date after a few days. How do you help them maximize their profitability during that time? How do you let brokers know who is calling in and what his

portfolio looks like so that they can leverage that knowledge? These are the types of problems we discuss with executives in an effort to become involved in setting the future direction.

Competitor Drivers

Competitors are another significant source of pressure for the executive. There are the long-established rivals who engage in a tug-of-war over a few percentage points of market share each year. There's a perennial stream of hungry new entrants with low overheads and niche expertise who poach the most lucrative contracts using the lure of price, flexibility, or innovation. There are disgruntled staff who resign, set up as competitors, and take a few plum accounts with them. There's even unexpected competition when a large company whose brand resonates in one industry decides to expand their footprint into new industries. Any insight you can offer on ways to remain competitive without dropping their price or cutting corners on quality will never go out of style with executives. Also, while they immerse themselves in their own company affairs, the fact that you sell to many companies places you in a unique position to offer something those executives are always looking for: insight into marketplace trends. Help them see beyond their silo walls to learn how other companies are solving the same competitor drivers they face.

Globalization Drivers

Globalization affects executives in a variety of ways. As they face competition from cheaper labor and production abroad, they risk losing market share. Consequently, to remain competitive, they must either drive cost out of their domestic infrastructure or outsource production and services to low-cost offshore providers. Either course of action creates risk as well as opportunity. How do they find the right production and distribution partners? How do they drive risk out of an extended supply chain and hedge for multiple currencies? How do they recruit and keep the right people? How will customers in different countries enjoy a uniform customer experience? How will staff members in different countries experience a consistent company culture that still resonates locally? If globalization means closing domestic factories, how will they manage labor laws, public relations, and finances? Do they have products that appeal to multiple markets? Does their brand play correctly when translated into other languages? (Ford faced this challenge when it discovered that *Pinto* translated as "young chicken" in Portuguese. Chevrolet's *Nova* translated as "it doesn't go" in Spanish. When Coca-Cola launched in China, it first used *Kekou-kela* which translated as "female horse stuffed with wax").

Helping executives anticipate and navigate regulatory issues is a tremendously valuable contribution, but to do so, you need to have studied the company's situation and weighed the company's options as judiciously as though you were on its board—that's the value executives are looking for.

Regulatory Drivers

In response to corporate scandals, industry reform, the advent of new technology, political correctness crusades, or shareholders and governments demanding greater transparency, new legislation is regularly introduced in different countries, industries, and professions.

If you can show how your solution helps an executive stay compliant with regulations, avoid fines, and keep out of jail, they'll listen, because C-Suite leaders run scared at the thought of being held personally accountable for regulatory and ethical breaches outside their control.

In 2016, John Stumpf lost his job as CEO of Wells Fargo after a corporate scandal in which thousands of the bank's employees opened more than two million fake bank accounts to give the appearance of meeting their sales targets. Yahoo CEO Marissa Mayer had her pay docked by $14 million and the company's head lawyer Ron Bell lost his job over a massive data breach involving hundreds of millions of user accounts in 2016. Such stories exist in every country.

Regulatory standards have always been part of business, but attention to them escalated when the Sarbanes-Oxley Act came into action and demanded greater disclosure. From 2012–2016, forced executive turnover due to ethical or regulatory lapses increased 36 percent over the previous five years.[4]

In 2018, "the most lobbied piece of legislation in history,"[5] the EU's General Data Protection Regulation (GDPR), will radically overhaul the relationship businesses have with personal data through a raft of new obligations and consumer rights. A Chief Information Security Officer spoke of the rising pressure of being "responsible for something they can never provide 100 percent assurance on, i.e., securing the enterprise. All it takes is one missed vulnerability, one insider, or one accidental insecure process."[6]

Damaging stories about regulatory or ethical breaches now travel fast and are repeated through the megaphone of 24/7 news cycles and online media. When these stories break, boards treat their company's reputation very seriously and can handle their executives harshly in an effort to restore shareholder confidence.

Come up with a solution that can help an executive avoid ethical or regulatory failure, or fix it quickly, and you'll always gain an audience.

In most sales situations, if you do research on the ways in which the six external drivers affect your customer, it will serve as a trail of breadcrumbs that leads to the people inside the organization most affected by those drivers—those with skin in the game who have the most to gain or most to lose.

As you set up meetings with these people, ask how the external drivers affect their internal operational and financial "bones." Do the drivers create opportunities or threats? How does the company plan to flex its corporate "muscles" to respond? What is the executives' sense of urgency and priority? Then show how you can help.

If you don't research these issues, you won't be able to talk about them. This leaves you at the Commodity Supplier level of sales proficiency, where any attempt to meet executives is perceived as an interruption. But by taking the time to understand what's going on in your customer's world and preparing informed opinions, you're adopting a habit of the Trusted Advisor.

Of course, beyond their industry, company, and personal drivers are the issues that generally affect the executive because of the office they hold (see Figure 3.2). These formal areas of accountability are unavoidable because they come with the job.

You can be confident that when you have studied the drivers affecting the executive's world, connecting them to the executive's role-specific issues will give context to the discussion and serve as an additional framework for positioning why your solutions are relevant.

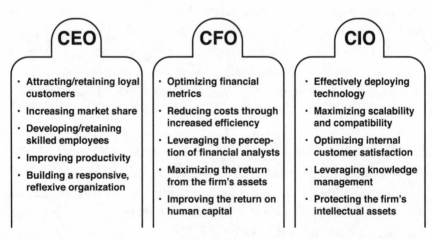

Figure 3.2 Role-Specific Issues Affecting Each CXO

CHAPTER SUMMARY

Let's summarize what we've discussed in this chapter by looking at the three key messages:

1. *Understand what motivates the executive.* Talk to the people who worked the account before you. Ransack the search engines. Look online for the executive's name as a speaker, conference delegate, or named source in a press release. See what issues she has risked her reputation on. Seek to understand how she made similar decisions in the past on the same subject or for contracts of a similar scope and size. If the executive is new to the role or is using it as a stepping-stone to better things, try to learn what triggers her interest and commitment. Is it purely a business outcome? Are there personal aspirations that need to be met? Is it about profits or people or position or power? If she's going to retire soon, find out what she wants to be remembered for, then help her get it. The point is, as the saying goes: "You can't sell John Smith what John Smith buys until you see through John Smith's eyes."

2. *Get into the game.* To stand out from a throng of me-too vendors, you must demonstrate your ability to be a business resource. This means doing more than parroting jargon in the hope that you'll sound the part. You need to know the specific business drivers that are motivating the executive's vision and be prepared to explore these and offer opinions and insights so that the contribution of your product or service can be put in context. In this way it will be clear that you have value to add that the executive wouldn't gain without a vendor or can't gain from one of your competitors. In other words, you have value that can be clearly differentiated from the status

quo *and* from other suppliers. If you got into the profession of business-to-business sales in an age when the fax machine spat out orders all day and times were good, or if your company brand and product quality drove sales to your door, you can be excused for never having mastered these skills and even being skeptical of the need for them. But how's that fax machine been performing for you lately? Don't make the mistake of denying the need for personal change, or you'll be wonderfully equipped . . . for a world that no longer exists.

3. *Right message, right audience.* No executive will spend money that he doesn't have to. His golden handshake depends on the profit and the share price achieved on his watch, so saving money—not spending it—will be a reflex for many, especially for those with a conservative accounting background who know that profit is made by increasing income or decreasing costs, with the lowest-risk action being to slash costs, delay expenditures, and cut heads. So if you're selling an idea for improving efficiency to conservative executives, frame your argument in terms of time, money, and saved resources. If you're selling an idea for raising quality to pragmatic executives, explain the quantitative and qualitative benefits of doing so. If you're selling an idea that helps your customer make more money, be sure you have the right audience of visionary or innovative executives. The right message will fall flat with the wrong audience. This is why it's so important to do your homework not only on the business issues, but on the people you're selling to as well.

Chapter 4

How to Find the Relevant Executive

Gaining a first meeting with senior-level executives is relatively straightforward for most professional salespeople with a bit of preparation and personal chutzpah. However, gaining return access to those same executives again and again is the real art. Executives don't waste time with people who add no value. More challenging still is building the type of trusted relationship where the executive will call you to discuss issues that are unrelated to anything you might be selling, but that are on her mind and that she hopes you will have insight into because she respects you as someone who has the pulse of the market. This chapter reveals how to develop this type of rapport in ways that come across as authentic and genuine because it shines through that you have the executive's best interests at heart.

We asked salespeople who cover a portfolio of small- and medium-size enterprises how they reach executives in those companies. By eliminating times known to be set aside for internal meetings and learning something about the executive's personal schedule, some salespeople are able to discover answers as precise as, "Tuesday mornings from 7:30 to 8:15 a.m., or every second Friday at 4 p.m. at the golf course." They have it down to a tee! These salespeople also confirm that in medium-size companies, it is often the owner-operator executive who turns off the lights at night—so a call that is placed after working hours is likely to be answered by the executive directly, or by a front desk security guard who will typically transfer your call right through.

We asked salespeople who cover a portfolio of large enterprises how they reach executives in those companies. A typical description of that environment is:

> You need a road map to navigate the maze of presidents, senior vice presidents, vice presidents, junior executives, directors, consultants, and various other chiefs. And even when you've figured out whose department a project resides in, there's no

guarantee that you can find who owns the pain. Plus you must contend with an army of personal assistants whose job it is to protect their boss's calendar from anyone who's not already on the approved list.

However, most of these salespeople agreed that an executive's assistant hears his boss on the phone all day, attends many of the same meetings, and understands what's topical and what a valuable idea looks like. Therefore, courting the assistant as though he were the executive himself shows respect for the role he plays and often opens doors that might otherwise remain closed.

And there are always examples of personal ingenuity. Here are two:

- *A computer hardware salesperson* whose territory spanned the area from Seattle to Salt Lake City to San Diego recalls that at one company, while he waited in the lobby for his appointments, he watched how people leaving the building treated the receptionist with respect as they walked out the door. The receptionist at this company was a mature lady who was always immaculately dressed and coiffured, and everybody, regardless of rank, made a point of nodding or talking with Barbara.

  One day this salesperson asked a mentor about the unusual deference people were paying, and he learned that Barbara was the company's fourth-largest shareholder and one of its original founders. She had traded a corner office for the front desk, where she could be the first face that greeted customers and could hear all the unguarded conversations that vendors and partners had in the lobby. Barbara served as a sentinel to protect her company's interests, and she had a direct line to all her executive peers. Needless to say, the salesperson in question cultivated a cordial relationship with Barbara, and shared his ideas on initiatives that he felt her company would benefit from. Accordingly, his ability to meet that company's executives increased.

- *A supplier of software* to a telecommunications company was so frustrated by what she described as "the high level of dysfunction, politics, and ass covering" in her client's business that she wrote a 30-page report titled "20 Reasons Why Selling to You Sucks." Maybe she'd watched Tom Cruise deliver his mission statement in *Jerry Maguire* one too many times. But she cared about her client as much as she cared about her quota, and she could not restrain herself. She printed only one copy, bound it in a faux leather cover, and hand-delivered it in a large envelope.

The next two weeks felt like an eternity. Every morning she expected her sales director to call her in to account for her impulsiveness. She began to wonder if she'd done the right thing. Sixteen days later, she received a phone call inviting her to lunch with the customer CEO. After exchanging pleasantries, he asked her two questions: "Are you confident that what you wrote is accurate?" to which she told him she was. Then he asked, "Why are you telling me things that even my own staff members don't admit to?" to which she replied that, while she did not know the answer, she was sure that this lack of communication was getting in the way of the company's moving forward. The CEO agreed, and within two months he had seconded this outspoken salesperson to his company for six months, granting her a roving commission and wide powers to root out the problems and initiate change.

In return, the salesperson's company would be given any contract it wanted to bid on during that six-month period, and her company made hundreds of thousands of dollars from the arrangement. Unsurprisingly, the salesperson accepted a full-time role in her client's company after the six months were over so that she could finish what she'd started, but her successor in the sales role continued to enjoy several years of prosperity because his predecessor had had the courage to give an executive something to really think about. Executives love to be challenged and solve problems when salespeople serve as peers instead of hucksters.

In asking salespeople who call on small, medium-size, and large companies how they reach executives, we found that, while tales like the ones just given provide some anecdotal value, they are not as valuable as hearing from C-level executives themselves.

The executives we talked to in our research projects complained about receiving too many calls from "people who think I ought to be involved in every purchase. It's a real aggravation because they are selling above where they need to be, and they clearly don't understand or care about how our process operates." Calling on the wrong executive not only wastes the time and resources of salespeople, but also damages their credibility and their chances of a future relationship with that executive.

IDENTIFYING THE RELEVANT EXECUTIVE

Competitive salespeople don't waste people's time, least of all their own. They identify the *relevant executive* for each sales opportunity, and they take time to understand the dynamics of their customer's organization to uncover where influence, power, and control over a particular project reside. "It doesn't have to be the CEO of a corporation," said one respondent. "It could be someone who has great influence with very little formal rank." We are reminded of Barbara the receptionist.

To determine the right person to target, focus first on the project or application that's associated with your sales opportunity. Then try to identify the highest-ranking executive who stands to *gain the most* or *lose the most* as it relates to the outcome of that project or application (see Figure 4.1).

Which executive should we align with in the customer organization?

The executive who stands to **gain the most** or **lose the most** as it relates to the outcome of the project or application associated with the sales opportunity.

This is the **relevant** executive for the sales opportunity—and that executive will possess **informal power**.

Figure 4.1 Defining the Relevant Executive

Typically, this is the relevant executive for the sales opportunity and the person you want to align with because that person possesses informal power that can be exercised over the buying decision. In fact, even if a buying decision has been made as part of the formal decision-making process, the relevant executive can usurp that decision because of the informal power they possess.

To further determine the right person to target, executives suggest that salespeople ask two additional questions.

"Who Will Really Evaluate, Decide, or Approve the Decision?"

An executive who initiates a project often reserves the decision-maker or approver role before she hands down the role of evaluating vendors to others. By way of definition, a *decision maker* is the person who analyzes the results of a formal team of evaluators, listens to recommendations, and then makes the final commitment to a vendor or to a certain course of action. There is usually one decision maker who makes that commitment.

On the other hand, an *approver* is usually a more senior person who reserves the right to review and approve or veto the decisions made by the decision maker. If the decision maker owns the budget and is trusted to make choices that are in the company's interests, the approver serves to offer objectivity but typically rubber-stamps what the decision maker wants to do. If the decision maker is new, under scrutiny, or about to leave the company, the approver's role becomes more active to safeguard the right decision.

Anyone above the person you have identified as the relevant executive, who is not involved in the project or is not affected by it, is not an appropriate contact. Anyone below this person does not have a broad enough view of the project, can give you bad or misleading information, and through ignorance of the issues can even extend the sales cycle unnecessarily.

"Who Has the Highest Rank and Greatest Influence?"

Every company has the formal structure of leaders and followers, ranks and reporting lines. You see the structure and ranks printed in annual reports and on people's business cards. It's the legitimate chain of command that companies need in order to preserve order and divide labor, and it is easy to identify. Some people obsess about climbing that hierarchy as a means of securing wealth, power, and control. But if rank works as a constant, do eight vice presidents in the same company all exert identical levels of influence? Rarely. Influence is the informal, political power that people wield. It rarely maps along the lines of a formal hierarchy, which makes it difficult to see. In reality, it operates exactly like a personal currency in that it rises and falls with how much of it is *created, stored, borrowed, consolidated, exchanged,* or *spent.* It is also affected by the relative influence of others in the community.

Do you have difficulty determining the relevant executive for your sales opportunities? This story serves as instruction.

Mike had been calling on the Medical Technology Director of a very large healthcare company for some time. He continually chased his target executive in an attempt to sell his solution, but to no avail. He then arranged for a meeting with the Technology Director and his boss, the Chief Medical Officer. This was achieved under the auspices of his own Regional Manager wanting to meet with a senior executive at that organization, which made a peer-to-peer meeting appropriate. This is a tried-and-tested door-opening tactic used the world over.

Mike and his boss flew into town for the meeting, but a snowstorm prevented the Medical Technology Director from attending. The CMO suggested they go ahead anyway. They discussed the client's needs, explained their solution, and reviewed the value proposition. After this, the CMO asked, "Why haven't we implemented this solution already, and what can I do to move it forward?"

The salesperson learned he was now dealing with the *relevant executive*—the CMO—and the Medical Technology Director with whom he had the prolonged relationship was actually an *irrelevant executive* who clearly didn't know what his boss valued, so hadn't brought these ideas to his attention.

With access now achieved with a *relevant executive*, and having established credibility with him, Mike could now contact this higher level for other opportunities in that organization.

The key here is that *irrelevant executives* will never tell you that they are irrelevant. They think they're a big wheel. They'll make you jump through hoops to prove how important they are. They even compartmentalize and restrict information from reaching their peers and superiors. You cannot allow the attainment of your sales quota (or target) to depend on these people. If you feel you're being blocked, you owe it to yourself and the executives of your customer's organization to find a way to break through to the upper levels. In our research, executives were most adamant about this. If you have value to offer that they will never hear about unless you circumvent a lower-level blocker, you should find a way to do so. Don't fret about the consequences of going over someone's head if that head is stuck in the sand. Chances are their boss knows it already and will reward you for getting past the roadblock.

There was a time when IBM's revenues declined sharply and the company faced its first-ever loss, which was also the largest in US corporate history to that point. The CEO left and Lou Gerstner was recruited from RJR Nabisco to take his job. This was the first time in IBM's history that a CEO had been recruited from outside the company. One of Gerstner's first observations as a fresh pair of eyes was that IBM salespeople had not learned the concept of the *relevant executive*. In his book, *Who Says Elephants Can't Dance: Inside IBM's Historic Turnaround*, Gerstner says: "Overall, the tasks we were being asked to take on were spreading beyond the domain of the CIO and into every corner of business operations—places where IBM had not, in general, ventured and where we lacked strong customer relationships."[1]

Gerstner saw that IBM salespeople were comfortable dealing with customer executives in the CIO silo but not as comfortable interfacing with the relevant executives in the functional areas of a business. So he became the company's top salesperson, repairing bonds with former customers, creating relationships with new ones, and maintaining relationships with IBM's largest customers. During his first year as CEO, Gerstner spent nearly 60 percent of his time with customers, becoming a role model for his direct reports, and showing the IBM salesforce how it was done.[2]

Before a leader joined from the outside, IBM may to some extent have suffered from a common malady you see in engineering-led companies that become "product proud." Leaders and salespeople spend time with customers who themselves wax lyrical about the product. The resulting echo chamber can make the product sound bigger and better than it really is compared to rival offerings, which is when salespeople can turn a deaf ear to an executive's unique needs. IBM wisely recognized this in time to avoid the trap. In a market of lookalike products, it changed the rules to build a reputation not just on great products but also on building a global professional services organization. This differentiated it from the product-centric vendors. Hence the slogan, "Nobody ever got fired for buying IBM," was born.

Selling to the executive level requires the same wisdom. If your marketing and sales literature or your company induction training focused you more on the products and services your company sells than the problems they solve for executives, beware. Selling value to executives requires a different cadence and content that is far more client-centric.

The first step to making this leap up the food chain is recognizing if you're spending too much time with lower-level buyers, on product-centric conversations, using presentations, and in discussions where more than half the conversation is about you and what you sell rather than the customer and what issues they face. Honestly, when you look at your marketing materials, sales presentations, and the past month of meetings or calls you've attended, are you talking more about your company, product, and benefits or more about emerging trends and issues that represent relevant and provocative value to the executive? Do this, and you'll become a true player—someone who builds influence with executive buyers. Since influence is a key currency you trade in when selling to the C-Suite, it warrants a closer look.

THE DYNAMICS OF ORGANIZATIONAL INFLUENCE

People *gain influence* and control from their level of involvement in and value to a discussion or project (*created*), by past contributions that still confer a level of credibility and respect (*stored*), by powerful people or brands they are associated with or anointed by (*borrowed*), and by how popular a person or idea becomes and the level of support and number of people who back it (*consolidated*).

People *lose influence* and control when the people or more influential brands that they were associated with go away or fall from grace, whereupon the influence that was borrowed or consolidated reverts to the amount of influence a person holds on his own (*exchanged*). People also lose influence by making mistakes, making enemies, or simply becoming has-beens whose stored supply of influence is depleted (*spent*).

As Janet Jackson crooned on her third album (coincidentally titled *Control*), we should all ask ourselves, "What have you done for me lately?" and take stock of our personal currency with the various stakeholders we want to be involved with, inside and outside the business arena. This is because influence doesn't have much of a shelf life. It doesn't store well.

So how do you identify a relevant executive who (1) is involved in a buying decision, (2) has a personal interest in the outcome, (3) has adequate rank to affect the formal decision process, and (4) has sufficient influence to affect the informal decision process? Executives we interviewed told us that there are four things to look for:

- *What people have done* (their track record)
- *What people do now* (their value)
- *Whom people know* (their network)
- *Their ability to drive change* (their will)

Their Track Record

Psychologists will tell you that the most reliable indication of future performance is past performance. People who have influence have a track record of consistent success. This doesn't mean that they are *always* successful. It means that they are *consistently* successful. When you hear that someone is "on a roll" or enjoying "a lucky streak" or that her "stars are in alignment," watch closely and you'll see that "success begets success." Success has a muscle memory, so when people enjoy success in one area of their life, they leverage their value and their network of associates to exert their will on their surroundings across several fields. That's influence. When you are trying to identify the relevant executive, look for patterns of success or lack of success in an individual's personal or work history. People with no track record have no currency to invest in the influence game.

Their Value

People build their track record in a number of different ways, but the key to maintaining it over time is creating value for their company, its executives, their customers, their peers, their partners, and other stakeholders. That's what you get recognized for; that's where you gain a reputation. The value may be personal and qualitative, such as introducing someone to a new idea or a topical book or news article, introducing him to people in your network who can help him, or simply bringing him useful information. Or the value may be commercial and quantitative. But as stated earlier, the influence you gain from these moments of glory soon fades once time outweighs the impact of your past contribution.

Value is, therefore, an everyday pursuit. You need to keep the iron hot. When you are trying to identify the relevant executive, look for the people who understand and can articulate what value looks like to their company, who are also contributing to delivering that value—as validated by their name being linked to all the right projects and talked about in all the right circles. Look for the people who are regarded as movers and shakers. If they are perceived as creating value, have a decent track record, and are connected to the sale you hope to make, they're candidates for being the relevant executive.

Their Network

The next marker we look for is each person's network: her tribe, grapevine, posse, alma mater, or power base. People who build influence are always plugged in to an informal chain of command, serving as either the hub or one of the spokes. They recognize their own limitations and surround themselves with people who can compensate for those limitations and balance them out. For example, new staff members who understand how influence works will connect with the alpha dog to learn the ropes and gain protection or favor. Old-timers will always nurture their allies inside and outside of their organization to stay current. Just as in the adage "birds of a feather flock together," sometimes these networks are made up of people who went to college or an MBA course together, were past colleagues in another company, or worked together on various projects in the same company. People tap into these networks for information, for advice, and for favors. All members of a network are bound by mutual advantage, what the Chinese call the rule of *guanxi*.

Easily understood as "I'll scratch your back, then you scratch mine," *guanxi* (pronounced *guan-shee*) is a fundamental tenet in Asian cultures whereby people become trusted as "insiders" through the mutual exchange of information, favors, or other forms of value. According to Luo Yadong's book *Guanxi and Business* (World Scientific Publishing Company, 2007), the Mandarin word *guan* originally meant "a door"; combined with *xi* its extended meaning is "to close up," meaning that behind the embrace of the closed door, you may be "one of us," but outside the door, your existence is barely recognized.

People who are "inside the door" of a network know about events before they happen; they're connected. In Italy there is a phrase for this: *radio scarpa*. The literal translation means "shoe radio," and the colloquial etymology refers to people who know what's going on simply by walking around, as though their very shoes could decode signals from every office in the company via the floorboards. Understanding this, a shrewd salesperson will know that if she doesn't know who the relevant executive is, or cannot reach him, the best approach is to broadcast her value to people on the grapevine. Sooner or later her message will reach the relevant executive.

To identify these players, always look for the people whose names are linked to many projects and discussions; look for the people who attend meetings and say very little, but whose few questions demonstrate deep insight that's beyond what they've heard from you; look for the people whose opinions others defer to, regardless of their rank; look for the people who seldom act surprised when they hear breaking news.

Without support from an executive's allies, it can be difficult to gain access.

Their Will

People with influence exert their will on the company; they set things in motion and change the status quo, and people follow them. But they seldom do it from their first day on the job. When a person joins a business, he learns how things work within the culture—how decisions are made, how ideas are discussed, even how people generally dress and speak. The way it works in business is the same way it works in college: you assimilate and work within a culture, or you get branded as an outsider. People build influence by first acclimating to the pervading belief system of how things should work (the company's *philosophy*) and working within the rules (the company's *policies*).

A former executive of Telecom New Zealand (now Spark New Zealand) who was given the task of driving business transformation in a company that was resistant to change recalls:

> You can't afford to scare the horses, or they'll bolt and you'll never catch them. Even though you're the only white horse in the herd, you must throw on a blanket that makes you look like a brown horse, and get close to all the other brown horses

so that they get to know you. Over time, you can let the blanket drop until they see that you're a white horse. But by then you've eaten the same hay and galloped in the same fields long enough that the horses have learned to trust you as one of their own. And of course, when the right horses neigh in your favor, the rest of the herd follows.

He first operated within the philosophy and policies of his company, created value, built a track record, and developed his network with various stakeholders so that he could drive change that would be supported.

This is how people with influence exert their will. When they have enough support from the right people, they can begin to interpret company policies as soft guidelines instead of hard rules, and find ways to change those policies for the benefit of the business. When a person reaches this level of influence, their personal philosophies start to be manifested in official ways, regardless of their official rank.

Donald T. Regan (1918–2003) was a tough-talking Wall Street financier appointed by US president Ronald Reagan as chief of staff, a role he was ousted from in February 1987. In his tell-all book *For the Record: From Wall Street to Washington* (Harcourt, 1988), Regan revealed that First Lady Nancy Reagan regularly consulted with astrologer Joan Quigley, and their exchanges shaped government policy as a result of Nancy's pillow talk with the president. Regan blamed his being fired on the first lady and her tarot card reader, neither of whom held any official rank, but who had plenty of influence. He writes: "Virtually every major move and decision the Reagans made during my time as White House chief of staff was cleared in advance with a woman in San Francisco who drew up horoscopes."

Dèng Xiǎopíng (1904–1997) never held office as head of state, but he served as de facto leader of the People's Republic of China from 1978 to the early 1990s. He was widely regarded as having backroom control without official rank. UN Secretary-General Kofi Annan said that Deng was the "primary architect of China's modernization and dramatic economic development,"[3] which included the revitalization of Shanghai's Pudong New Area as China's new economic hub and the foundation for China's eventual entry into the World Trade Organization, which significantly changed the global economy.

Karl Rove (1950–) ran a company that managed direct mail, telephone polling, and fund-raising; according to the *Atlantic* magazine,[4] he was the primary strategist for 41 statewide, congressional, and national races between 1981 and 1999, of which his candidates won 34. That's a lot of friends in high places. He was appointed by George H. W. Bush to advise on the 1980 presidential campaign, in which Rove was fired midcampaign for leaking information. Such was Rove's influence that he was rehired to handle direct mail for the 1984 Reagan-Bush and 1992 Bush presidential campaigns, from the latter of which he was fired again for leaking information. He returned to advise George W. Bush in his campaign to become governor of Texas in 1994, in his 1998 reelection campaign, and in his 2000 and 2004 presidential campaigns. Following the 2004 US presidential election, Bush referred to Rove as "the architect" because of his role in taking Bush to the White House. Rove later came to be regarded as "Bush's brain" and the real power behind the throne.[5] It is unlikely that Rove could have exerted his will without his track record, his value, and his network, all of which he had carefully assembled throughout his career.

But this cuts both ways. Some people in high-ranking positions are revealed to have little influence at all. Colin Powell (1937–) was named national security adviser to US President Ronald Reagan in 1987 and chairman of the Joint Chiefs of Staff by President George H. W. Bush in 1991. During the Gulf War he served as chief military strategist, and his popularity soared to the extent that he was courted by political parties to run for office. He declined but was persuaded to serve as secretary of state under President George W. Bush in 2000. By all appearances Powell had power and influence. He had the rank, the title, and the accolades.

However, by the end of 2001 people started to question if he had any real power at all. His face featured on the September 10, 2001 cover of *Time* magazine above the headline, "Where Have You Gone, Colin Powell?" It was apparent someone else in Bush's White House was calling the shots for decisions that belonged to Powell's office. That person was Condoleezza Rice, a White House executive who had the ear of the President. She spoke to Bush nearly every day, talked sports, worked out with him, and often accompanied the Bush family to Camp David on weekends. Her personal relationship allowed for influence over decisions above her pay grade. And the rule of thumb when it comes to influence is that what you represent informally will eventually be ratified formally. Unsurprisingly, she was appointed Secretary of State in President Bush's second term, thus claiming both formal and informal power.

People without influence lack the power to work outside the boundaries set by others and must view policies as rules that cannot be broken. People with influence can interpret and modify an organization's rules as though they were mere guidelines. While others might be punished for doing so, those who are influential routinely have their acts legitimized as correct under the circumstances of the moment.

So, to learn which people have influence, we must profile the stakeholders in a customer's business, looking at all these factors. When we do this, front-runners quickly and clearly come into focus. But beware: Multiple people can all have various levels of influence. The final question we must address is: "Which person is most influential with regard to this sale?"

To find the answer to this, we explored whether there are degrees of influence and how to tell the difference between them. Company executives and successful account managers confirmed that influence is like energy—most of the time the influence of the people you're selling to lies dormant as stored or potential energy. It's not until something happens that the potential energy is released as kinetic energy and is set in motion to act upon the environment. It's in times of change that a person's influence is most apparent.

For example, when a new policy says that managers must obey a hiring freeze, but one department continues to hire without adverse consequences, this may indicate that the manager has enough influence to treat the rules that others must abide by as mere guidelines. When your customer undergoes a restructuring, a merger, or an acquisition, watch closely who consolidates his power or has new roles created for him, compared to those who see their empires unravel. Often those changes appear as a flash of lightning in the night sky, when everything is suddenly illuminated. Changes like that don't happen overnight or without prior discussion; people either *decide* what should happen, *make* those things happen, or *wonder* what happened.

Those who decide what happens are usually the most influential. These people control outcomes and shape what happens by defining the organization's goals and objectives. They surround themselves with trusted lieutenants who serve as their eyes, ears, and arms to make things happen. Because of their connections, they understand what is going on before it occurs, can anticipate what changes are taking place, and avoid the traps and dead ends that others blunder into.

Because influence doesn't follow the hierarchical lines of authority, it is possible for a junior staff member who has huge subject matter expertise to be at the hub of a decision-making process, enlisting a higher-ranked boss to legitimize her ideas by creating or rewriting a formal project. This is an example of influence flowing up from subordinate to superior. It can also flow sideways from peer to peer, and, as established earlier, external parties holding no rank at all can exert influence on a group. Influence can also flow from the boss down to the members of his staff, although when this happens it is more difficult to know whether you're watching the effect of influence or simply rank at work.

We might picture this informal structure as three concentric circles, as seen in Figure 4.2.

The inner circle (those who decide what happens) holds the highest influence and is surrounded by its network of allies and trusted resources (who make things happen for those in the inner circle). On the periphery is everyone else who gets involved in a project solely because formal roles require it. These people typically wield power only in proportion to their titles.

The closer to the center someone is located, the more influence that person holds. It's here that the relevant executive for any sales opportunity will be found, for the inner circle is composed of those people who typically find ways to initiate projects that require funding and who have the most to gain or lose based on the outcomes. Like the modern-day parable that in a plate of bacon and eggs, the chicken is only a participant, whereas the pig is fully

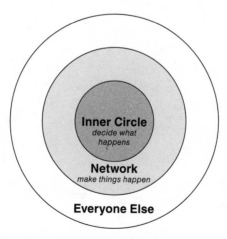

Figure 4.2 Degrees of Influence

committed, so it is with those relevant executives in the inner circle who have skin in the game.

Because influence is situational, the people you find in the inner circle and their network will change from opportunity to opportunity. It's important for you to understand this, because some salespeople we have consulted fall into the trap of mapping the politics and influence in their key accounts for one deal and then expecting those things to remain constant in the next deal. Influence is always in motion as a by-product of the nature of each opportunity and of who needs to be involved in the buying process, the incumbency of current suppliers, who wants to preserve those suppliers and who wants to replace them, whether a project fits within a department's discretionary spending levels or needs to be escalated, and the fact that people fall into and out of favor all the time. People may leave, and new people with allegiances of their own may be hired. There are so many variables that we recommend that you profile influence one opportunity at a time.

Once you've identified the right executive to sell to, the next question is how to gain access.

CHAPTER SUMMARY

Let's summarize what we've discussed in this chapter. Here are several key points:

1. *Identify the relevant executive.* Simply put, the *relevant executive* is the executive who stands to *gain the most* or *lose the most* as it relates to the outcome of the project or application associated with your sales opportunity. This is the one person who most feels the pain and has skin in the game. If a project to find a supplier is already underway, the relevant executive is the person who first identified the need and had the credibility to turn it into a formal project backed by resources. If you're trying to create a project by tapping into a problem that the customer needs to solve, the relevant executive will be the person who has the most to gain or the most to lose. Many stakeholders will need to be met and developed as supporters. But at the center of the web is the executive who is most relevant to this decision. They may not always be at the very top of the company, so sell only as high as you need to. But a general rule of thumb is: *The bigger the pain, the higher the game.*

2. *Confirm your view of the relevant executive.* Examine the four building blocks of influence, namely:
   • What has that executive done (their track record)?
   • What does that executive do now (their value)?
   • Who does that executive know (their network)?
   • What is that executive's ability to drive change (their will)?

   Recheck your view that the relevant executive you have identified reflects those building blocks of influence. Then, look for ways to align with the relevant executive so that you can advance the relationship and have that executive selling for you in your absence. That's right. Even when you're not present, if you have convinced the relevant executive that you can create significant value for her, she will sell in your absence.

3. *Sort out the irrelevant executive(s).* You may have been comfortable calling on numerous executives in the customer organization; however, you might determine that these "executives" are really only lower-level buyers who can't make the key buying decision. Remember, irrelevant executives will never tell you that they are irrelevant. Watch for the signs that they're an empty suit, and find ways around them. Be reminded of the salesperson calling on the Medical Technology Director who only learned that the Director was irrelevant because of a snowstorm!

Chapter 5

How to Gain Access to the C-Suite

According to our research with C-level executives, the most effective way to gain access is through a recommendation by someone in the executive's company (see Figure 5.1). A full 84 percent of executives said that they would *usually* or *always* grant a meeting with a salesperson who was recommended internally. This highlights the importance of building companywide relationships that open doors to senior management.

Other methods did not fare as well. Referrals from outside the organization are sometimes successful, yet more than half of executives will never or only occasionally meet with a salesperson who has been recommended by an outside contact. Cold calling ranked the lowest, with only 20 percent of participants saying that they would *usually* grant a meeting as a result, while 44 percent said that they would *never* respond to cold calls. A letter or e-mail sent before the call improves the odds only slightly.

With 84 percent of executives saying that they would *usually* or *always* meet a salesperson if that salesperson were recommended internally (87 percent in China), the study clearly indicates that establishing relationships at lower levels of the organization is critical before trying to access the executive's calendar. One CEO explained that he would grant a meeting "when I see or hear something that might be applicable in my world, or at the request of some of my cohorts around here."

	ALWAYS	USUALLY	OCCASIONALLY	NEVER
Recommendation from someone in your company	16%	68%	16%	0%
Referral from someone outside your company	8%	36%	44%	12%
A letter or e-mail, followed by a telephone call	4%	20%	40%	36%
Cold call by telephone	0%	20%	36%	44%
Contact at an off-site event	0%	44%	32%	24%

Figure 5.1 Scorecard of Methods for Gaining Access to Executives

These "cohorts" are part of the executive's influence network; they may be a friend of someone in the executive's inner circle, an internal consultant, or a low-level employee within the organization who just happens to have credibility with an inner-circle executive.

Competitive salespeople understand and work the influence networks within their customer's organization. "I'm always trying to find someone I can approach to mentor me and help maneuver my message through the account," said one sales executive. "I strive to build a win-win relationship by finding people who can benefit from this relationship. They actually sponsor your effort to reach senior executives."

Our China research provided scores with similar highs and lows, with a variance of plus or minus 3 percent. But in talking with directors of government-run enterprises, managers of private companies, and the executives of foreign-owned companies trading in China, we found some new reasons *why* Chinese executives prefer to meet salespeople only after they receive a recommendation from someone they trust.

To explain it, we're going to need a quick history lesson to help you understand where they're coming from. We include this because with China's projected rise in importance as a trading partner and employer this century, it's likely that at some point in your career China will affect some aspect of your sales ecosystem or supply chain relationships. Plus, it's fascinating.

UNDERSTANDING THE MINDSET OF CHINESE EXECUTIVES

Six hundred years ago, China was a political, an intellectual, a military, and an economic colossus. In his groundbreaking work *1421: The Year China Discovered America* (Harper, 2004), Gavin Menzies contrasts China's position on the fifteenth-century world stage with that of the major European powers of the time, and concludes that in every way, China ruled supreme:

At the inauguration of emperor Zhu Di's Forbidden City in Beijing on 2 February 1421, 26,000 dignitaries ate a 10-course banquet served on fabulous porcelain. At the feast to celebrate the coronation of Catherine of Valois as Queen of England on 21 February 1421, 600 guests ate one course of salted cod on slabs of stale bread that served as plates. Zhu Di's walled city was more than 1,400 times the size of the walled City of London. Later that year, King Henry VI went to war against France commanding an army of 5,000 men whom he ferried across the English Channel in four fishing boats. In the same year, Emperor Zhu had a standing army of 1,000,000 men.

The Emperor had more than 1,350 warships, 3,000 merchant vessels and 400 grain transports, plus an armada of 250 treasure ships equipped with cannons and rockets that transported 30,000 men around the world. Each ship was 400 feet long. By contrast, Columbus' Santa Maria was 82 feet long, about the size of one of Zhu's ship rudders.

The Silk Road was open all the way to Persia. China's industrial system was flourishing. Forward bases had been opened around the Indian Ocean. The way was clear for Zhu Di's greatest gamble yet—the entire world was to be brought into Confucian harmony.

Yet within 150 years, a change in policy saw China reverse its expansionist policies, scrap its navies, and burn its shipyards. It entered a long sleep, where it remained while other world powers emerged during the Industrial Revolution. In the 300 years that followed, China was embroiled in various wars and rebellions, mounting debts, the loss of Hong Kong to British rule, and the eventual end of 5,000 years of imperial rule. China first became a republic in 1912; this republic was overturned by a prime minister who declared himself the new emperor in 1915, then "died" a year later, leaving a power vacuum that was greedily filled by ruthless warlords who carved the country into fiefdoms.

After World War I, the revolutionary Sun Yat-Sen set out to unite his fragmented nation through an alliance with the Communist Party of China and with help from the Soviets. His protégé, Chiang Kai-shek, disagreed with communist rule and seized control of the rival Nationalist Party, using military force to defeat the southern and central warlords. He then waged war on the Communist Party itself in 1927 and drove its supporters to the northwest in what became known as the Long March, during which the communists reorganized under Chairman Mao Zedong. China then endured 14 years of tumult that included the Japanese invasion and World War II, during which time the communists succeeded in winning popular support. Facing oblivion, Chiang Kai-shek fled with his Nationalist Party to form the government of Taiwan in 1949, the same year that the People's Republic of China was formed as a new nation on the mainland. Today's tension between China and Taiwan originated here.

Chairman Mao instituted the Great Leap Forward, an attempt to lift the economy by mandating the production of steel in backyard furnaces, which Mao promised would turn China into a world-class steel producer to rival the United States and the United Kingdom. This was a massive financial and humanitarian disaster that saw the country denuded of trees and labor diverted from harvesting to melt pots and pans. Worthless cheap iron, famine, starvation, and around 40 million deaths were the result of this pipe dream. Mao stepped down in 1959 and was replaced by new leaders.

And China heard: "Don't believe promises, only facts."

In 1978 China became a market economy, and in 2001 it entered the World Trade Organization and opened its borders to foreign business. As the world shifted production to low-cost Chinese mills and factories, China became cash rich. In a bid to acquire the legitimacy of western marques, it has made partial or whole bids or acquisitions of major Western brands that include IBM's PC division, Motorola mobile phones, GE Appliances, European football club's Inter Milan, AC Milan and Aston Villa, Pirelli tires, British department store chains House of Fraser and Harvey Nichols, French clothing chain Sandro, Volvo, London Taxis, Gieves & Hawkes Tailors of London, Italian fashion brand Cerutti, Weetabix, Tommee Tippee feeding bottles, Club Med, vacuum cleaner brands Dirt Devil, Vax, and Hoover, Morgan Stanley, Standard Bank (South Africa), PetroKazakhstan, Fortis Insurance, Pizza Express, Swiss watch brand Rotary, Rio Tinto, MG Rover, Maytag, Marconi, Smithfield Foods, AMC Theatres, UK pharmacy chain Superdrug, French smartphone company Wiko, Sunseeker luxury yachts, the World Triathlon Corp (which owns the Ironman competition), and even the Grindr app.

According to a report by the Mergermarket Group, China hit a new annual high in its number of Western acquisitions and investments by August 2016, with 173 deals completed that year alone worth $128.7 billion. Among these were Tianjin Tianhai Investement Development Co. buying Ingram Micro for $6.3 billion; Qingdao Haier purchasing GE Appliances for $5.4 billion; ChemChina acquiring Swiss pesticide and seed producer Syngenta AG for $43 billion; Tencent buying Finnish mobile game developer Supercell for $8.6 billion; and Anbang Insurance acquiring Starwood Hotels (which owns New York's Waldorf Astoria) for $14.3 billion.

All of this is in line with China's State Council announcing in May 2015 that its official "Made in China 2025" strategy is to move up the value chain and avoid being pinched at one end by lower cost countries and at the other end by higher quality manufacturers around the world.[1]

Decades after Mao's communal privations, China's nouveau riche have responded to Deng's battle cry, "To get rich is glorious," going from nothing to everything in just a few years. In preparation for the 2008 Beijing Olympics and 2010 Shanghai World Expo, massive capital expenditures were made to modernize those cities. According to some sources, almost a quarter of the world's 150,000 construction cranes are now in China. As *Time* magazine journalist Hannah Beech writes:

> To be suddenly wealthy in China is to be engaged in a full-blown, keeping-up-with-the-Chans spending contest. In June, a Bentley sold for 8.8 million yuan ($1.06 million) at a Beijing auction—apparently because eight is a lucky number, not because the car was worth that amount. In the gambling paradise of Las Vegas, Chinese jet-setters have displaced Japanese industrialists as the most prevalent—and most welcome—group of high rollers. Chinese entrepreneurs don't tend to do the Jeff Bezos thing—dressing down in wrinkled khakis. *"In China, if you're rich, you have to look the part,"* says Wang Deyuan, who owns one of the top ad agencies in southern China. *"You have to show you have money, otherwise no one believes that you're rich."*[2]

And China heard: "If you can't see it, it isn't real."

"I'll believe it when I see it" is a common sentiment. This is a product of the executive wanting to remain at a safe distance in case things go pear-shaped; he can't lose face if the salesperson is managed through an intermediary. But once value is exchanged and future value is offered, a Chinese executive will be more willing to allow the relationship to be transferred. When this occurs, the person who referred the salesperson gains face under the rules of *guanxi*.

So the rule of thumb when trying to gain access to a Chinese executive is to be patient and work through trusted intermediaries until the executive is ready to deal directly. It can take a year—some say two—for the executive to see that you're in for the long haul. Your company brand can help you open doors, but ultimately it's the longevity of a personal relationship that executives are after, along with access to your personal network—again, *guanxi* at work.

If two vendors have a similar product, but one has a prestigious brand, association with the prestigious brand will win every time. If two vendors have similar products and equally prestigious brands, but one salesperson is known around town and has a strong network of associates, it's the relationship exchange that will win every time.

Think of it as one giant game of Facebook and LinkedIn, where your reputation and the people you know are as good as hard currency.

HOW DO EXECUTIVES SCREEN AND TEST SALESPEOPLE?

The first gauntlet you run when you're trying to meet any executive is the system of roadblocks that are put in place to preserve her calendar or diary. You must find a path through these screens and filters and then introduce yourself in a way that will cause the executive to give you a meeting.

Roadblocks don't exist just to make life difficult for salespeople. Most of the time a roadblock is a legitimate mechanism that has been put in place to help the executive focus on important tasks rather than distractions (see Figure 5.2).

Why Do Roadblocks Exist?

In some companies, getting calendar time with a senior executive may happen only if you contact the executive assistant or the executive's secretary. You simply can't get on the executive's calendar by contacting him directly. In that case, you may have to either use a sponsor or treat the assistant as a resource to help you schedule a meeting with the executive.

The chief causes of roadblocks are the following:

1. **Executives delegate meetings of this type.**
2. **It's the formal process used in this organization.**
3. **The executive is too busy to schedule meetings with external suppliers.**
4. **The executive's previous experience with salespeople suggests that they should be seen by lower-level executives first.**

Figure 5.2 Causes of Roadblocks

Getting Past the Roadblocks

We've provided a worksheet in Appendix B for planning how to bypass the roadblocks you face. The techniques that can be used to address them include the following:

- When there's an organizational change in your company, suggest having a meeting to explain the new structure.
- Suggest a meeting with an equivalent-level executive from your organization (like-rank selling) as shown in the example presented earlier in Chapter 4 (concerning the irrelevant executive).
- Accept redirections to meet other executives or people of lower rank, but always ask the executive to make an introduction and request a follow-up meeting to review the outcomes.
- Schedule a meeting with an executive to communicate past value delivered or to confirm your ongoing value.
- Contact the executive when there's any significant event in the customer's market, even if it's unrelated to the current sales campaign. Executives like to know that you're thinking about them, even if there's nothing for you to sell.

The stakes are high if you cannot access the relevant executive. Some of the latest data from companies whose sales cycles are nine months or more indicate that it may cost more than $200,000 to pursue an opportunity, whether you win or not.[3] That's a significant sum to bet on selling to low-level managers. If you don't have the chance to get past the gatekeepers and meet the relevant executive, it may be prudent to walk away and save the cost of sale.

There's one other word of caution that bears mentioning at this point: Don't attempt to circumvent the gatekeeper unless you have a high degree of confidence that you can obtain the meeting with the executive. As one savvy salesperson put it: "Hell hath no fury like a gatekeeper scorned!" Once she is around a roadblock, a salesperson will be quickly tested. CXOs told us that salespeople who get past their roadblocks on a cold call get five minutes to show that they can add value. Here are some tips:

- Speak from a business perspective and don't get caught up in the "bells and whistles" of product features.
- Raise relevant questions and share business perspectives that are new to the executive.
- If you're an incumbent, point out the potential limitations of your products in light of changing demands and provide ideas for making improvements, thus enhancing your credibility.

CHOOSING A PATH

After you've evaluated whether it's more advisable to work with the gatekeepers or to go around them, you'll need to decide how to navigate that path to the executive. How do you go from where you are today to gaining an audience? Most salespeople know at least four approaches for achieving access to senior executives (see Figure 5.3). As Figure 5.2 showed earlier, some of these approaches are more successful than others.

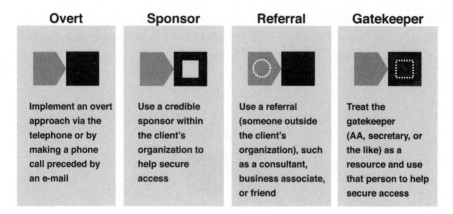

Overt	Sponsor	Referral	Gatekeeper
Implement an overt approach via the telephone or by making a phone call preceded by an e-mail	Use a credible sponsor within the client's organization to help secure access	Use a referral (someone outside the client's organization), such as a consultant, business associate, or friend	Treat the gatekeeper (AA, secretary, or the like) as a resource and use that person to help secure access

Figure 5.3 Tactics to Gain Access to Executives

Overt

An *overt* approach is one in which you contact the executive directly. This type of approach can be accomplished by a direct telephone call, or by a telephone call preceded by a letter or an e-mail. However, don't be surprised if the overt approach leads to your being sent down to lower levels. Our research revealed that 44 percent of executives would *never* respond to this approach, and only 36 percent said that they would respond *occasionally*.

Sponsor

With this approach, someone inside the client's organization helps you gain access. It's absolutely critical that the sponsor have credibility with the executive. In our research, executives said that this was the most effective way to secure access to them. In fact, 68 percent said that they *usually* grant an audience to salespeople sponsored by a credible person within their own organization, and 16 percent said that they *always* do so.

Referral

With the *referral* approach, someone outside the client's organization (such as a business associate, consultant, or friend of the executive) helps you secure access to the executive. In most cases, this is an effective way to reach the executive. As with a sponsor, the referral's credibility with the executive is critical to success.

Gatekeeper

Try treating gatekeepers as though they were the executives themselves. Explain your proposition and ask their opinions. The best executive assistants will be conversant with their boss's key business issues and will immediately see your value. The poor ones won't understand the discussion but may pass you forward because you *sound* like you belong. If you are successful in obtaining a gatekeeper's support, keep them in the loop as a matter of courtesy.

Executives interviewed confirm that gatekeepers can be extremely beneficial to salespeople if you treat them as an ally rather than someone to blow past on your way to the top. A salesperson received a call from an administrative assistant to the global director of marketing for a major company. The assistant went on to say that her boss was working on a white paper and wanted to cite some content that the salesperson had previously developed and had published. She wanted to know if the salesperson would allow the content to be used in a white paper that the director of marketing wanted to distribute within his firm. The salesperson worked with the assistant and only asked to review the white paper before it was distributed. After the project was completed and the white paper was distributed, the director contacted the salesperson directly and asked what he could do to help the salesperson and return the favor. Clearly the relationship had already become collaborative. The result was a series of introductions to other executives in the firm that led to a significant amount of business being generated over several years. All of this was possible because the gatekeeper had been treated as a resource—and more importantly, the gatekeeper had been treated as if she was the executive.

Executives are prone to ask secretaries, receptionists, and their assistants how you treat them, and if *they* trust you. The small talk you make with these people matters! Once you leave your car in the parking lot, step out of your Uber, or get off the subway, it's good policy to expect that everybody you meet is watching your every action. The closer you get to your destination, the denser the population of staff who work for your account. You never know if the person you encounter in the garage, lobby, restroom, or café is going to be someone who will make or break your deal. Treat everyone as important, and you can't go wrong.

INITIAL CONTACT WITH THE EXECUTIVE

In Appendix B, there is a template for an initial telephone call to the executive. You can use this template to help you prepare to contact the executive for the first time. It contains five simple steps:

1. Preparing Your Approach

Simply put, you want the executive to perceive you as being prepared, succinct, and confident. Most importantly, put yourself in the position of the executive as you prepare your approach. Imagine you are sitting on the other end of the telephone listening to your approach. In fact, after you have prepared and practiced your approach, call your own voice messaging system, then listen to yourself and ask: "Would you respond positively to this salesperson?"

Your initial telephone call should not last more than three or four minutes. Here's a tip: If you can determine an executive's personal agenda and satisfy it while also addressing her business agenda, you will have easily developed competitive differentiation.

2. Introduction

Begin with a brief introduction that clearly states who you are and why you're contacting the executive. Explain your connection to your sponsor or referrer, if appropriate. You have only one opportunity to make a good first impression! This is particularly important if this is your first meeting with the executive. You want to make certain the executive understands that you did some level of preparation prior to the meeting.

Remember, executives talk to many different people and organizations during their day. Don't assume they'll already be mentally disengaged from their previous meeting by the time they start talking with you. Salespeople know to "break the ice" at the start of a meeting. We do it to create a social bond. Another way of looking at it is that whatever meeting the executive just came from has frozen their thought process.

Your first task is to break through that frost, thaw their brain, and make their thought process malleable enough to be in the moment with you. So you offer a remark about some shared experience they can relate to, take them away from the workplace, then bring them back to it on terms you define. Make sure they know who you are, why you are calling, what outcomes your meeting will deliver, and what value this will be to them. Not only will their minds be ready for fresh input, but you'll have started capturing their heart as well.

3. Purpose

Explain the purpose of the call. You'll have to explain to the executive why you're calling him. This could be to arrange a meeting to discuss a specific business issue that you understand to be compelling to the executive. Paraphrasing what hundreds of senior executives told us consistently: "One of the single best ways for a salesperson to gain credibility at my level is to listen before proposing a solution. This is the number one trait I look for in salespeople I would consider as candidates to be one of my Trusted Advisors."

4. Credibility

Explain the homework you've done on the executive's organization, or perhaps cite the past value you've delivered to the organization if this call is to an executive in an existing account. In addition, use that homework to provide a glimpse of the future value you could deliver, given validation by citing how you've helped other companies address similar challenges. It's a potent combination.

5. Commitment to Action

Propose a clear and specific action or next step, such as the next meeting, bringing other people into the discussion, or asking the executive to share information only they can authorize. Executives like to be told what you expect them to do. No, really. The more directive you can be, and the more you ask of them, the more they see you as a peer. Executives report that too many salespeople ask them to do nothing, as if they're astonished they made it this far and don't want to push their luck. Don't be one of them. Go in with a plan. Have a set of next steps ready to request at the meeting with the executive. Hold them accountable for what they agree to do, just as you will be accountable for accomplishing what they ask of you. Quid pro quo.

Let's say you ask for a meeting over the phone and the executive refers you to someone at a lower level in the organization. This may not be the result you wanted, but it isn't a train wreck either. The executive may simply be referring you to someone in her network of advisors who is better suited to evaluate the discussion. It always helps to do three things:

1. Ask the executive for an introduction to the person, because this is far better than your having to call him cold. You can leverage the fact that his boss sent you to talk.
2. Ask her what she hopes you will achieve with her subordinate, and what additional people are suited to have the discussion with you. Turn it into a networking opportunity.
3. Ask to reconnect with the executive to review how what you hear and learn from her subordinates compares to the level of readiness in other companies for which you've solved the same problem. Executives typically like to know how their company benchmarks, so use the occasion to demonstrate your value as someone with insight beyond the executive's silo walls.

Here's what one sales professional shared about this topic:

My customer went through a management reorganization, which eroded some of my support base. I had a good relationship with the engineering manager who was promoted to COO when the former COO was promoted to CEO. I wanted to get close to the new CEO, so I called my contact for advice. The COO confirmed my ideas about the issues that were of most importance to the CEO and agreed to support my solution if I was successful in getting it positioned.

I then contacted the CEO and asked to meet with him. After explaining the ways I felt we could add value, he said it didn't make sense for us to meet unless I first had the support of a midlevel manager whom I'd never met and didn't know existed. I could have perceived this to be a negative outcome. But it was clear that this person's opinion mattered to the CEO: She was in his personal network. I did a thorough discovery of the firm's key business drivers, and after the meeting she sent an e-mail to the CEO suggesting that it was a good idea to discuss future opportunities in more detail.

This is a clear example of how being referred down can grant you credibility with other key players and in return enhance your credibility with the executive who sent you there in the first place.

Here's another. A new salesperson in his first territory attended a workshop and received a list of questions meant to position him as a consultant, not an order taker. He doubted he'd ever use them. He had little experience, no references to open doors, and felt like a failure. Why had his boss sent him to a class about techniques that were so obviously out of his reach? That night, he got on a train and found the only free seat was across from an executive he had been trying to meet for six months with no success.

He was some way into the journey before he summoned the nerve to strike up a conversation. After some small talk to break the ice and reset that executive's brain, the salesperson began asking some of the questions he remembered, not as a salesperson, but as a fellow business person who knew the executive's business and was curious about what made it tick. To the salesperson's delight, the executive was impressed with the interaction. He eventually asked the salesperson what he did for a living, and learned the young man was an account manager who had been trying to get an appointment for some time. With a wry smile he then pulled out a business card and said, "Well you won't wait much longer to get an appointment with me. I'd like you to be in my office at 10 a.m. tomorrow, so that we can continue this conversation." The salesperson was astonished, and e-mailed his trainer the same night.

There's more to the tale. Several months later, the sales trainer shared this story with another group of people from the same company. One of the managers spoke up and said:

> Would you like to know how that story ended? The salesperson's name is Marc, and, since that train ride home, he has closed two huge deals with this client. Before his training, we had never had a meeting with anyone in that company. Marc was the first to break through. Now we are in negotiations there on the biggest deal of the quarter. It will make Marc's quota for the whole year. He is now seen as a Trusted Advisor by that executive. He's even been introduced to other companies in that executive's network. Marc's entire outlook has changed from being a newbie who had no success, to seeing himself as an extension of the client's organization, and indispensable to their success. And it all started with the right questions.

With these tips, you're on your way to securing a first meeting with the executive even when you're making a cold call, albeit a well-researched one! However, if your company provides air support in the form of marketing campaigns designed to trouble the executive about business problems he faces that your company can solve, your chances of success are greatly magnified because the executive is already warmed up to recognize that he has the problem, and he already knows that your company plays in the space.

Whatever the approach, you're now ready to meet face to face, where the first item on your agenda is to establish your credentials and your credibility.

CHAPTER SUMMARY

Let's summarize what we've discussed in this chapter about the second question in our research: "How do salespeople gain access to executives?" Let's break it down to the top three messages:

1. *Determine which access method is best.* We discussed four approaches to gaining access, namely: the overt, sponsor, referral, and gatekeeper methods. Consider these options and develop the approach you think will provide you with the best outcome. When dealing with gatekeepers, treat the gatekeeper as a resource and take that a step further by treating the gate-keeper as if she was the executive herself.

2. *Get close to the influencers.* Every decision to buy from a supplier involves several evaluators, one decision maker, and possibly several approvers. This is the formal decision process. Outside of that, there are other people who get involved who have influence disproportionate to their role. Some of these may not even be in the customer's organization. Finding the *power behind the throne* and aligning your sale with his agenda is critical. If you win the formal vendor evaluation but you don't have political support, you might lose the deal. If you lose the formal vendor evaluation but you have powerful influencers on your side, the formal criteria will change to justify your winning. Nobody says this is fair, but it's how every large investment decision is made, even in government contracts. Learn and master these rules; they're the only ones that really matter.

3. *Navigate the roadblocks.* Executives test salespeople to see if they're worthy of an audience. Sometimes this is for sport,

but most times it's to protect their calendar from time wasters. Their organization will include project leaders, executive assistants, and others who will tell you to deal solely with them, tell you to go away, or leave you hanging while you wait for them to return your call. There are several options you can choose for getting past the roadblocks and even for converting the blockers into allies. When you choose to go around someone or over her head, you need to weigh the pros and cons of doing so based on the situation at hand. Research shows that using the telephone to cold call an executive is the least effective method, with an 80 percent failure rate. Gaining a referral from someone the executive trusts is the most effective, with an 84 percent success rate. If you have strong marketing support that regularly troubles the executive about the problems he is facing, the referral to meet you will usually come from the executive himself.

Chapter 6

How to Establish Credibility with the C-Suite

Salespeople we've both worked with in our respective consulting practices speak of a moment of terror that occurs after they've stormed the gates, swung a grappling hook at the tallest tower, and climbed the rope to the top. As they finally stand in front of their target executive, how do they establish their credentials so that they can avoid being thrown back out the window? This chapter reveals what executives have told us you can do to win the keys to the kingdom.

Executives use their first personal meeting with a salesperson to answer specific questions:

- Does the salesperson understand our needs? Has he done his homework on our key business drivers?
- Has he been able to convey how his product or service applies to me? Why it is better than his competitors'?
- Is this individual an empowered decision maker, or will he have to consult his manager for decisions?
- Is the salesperson professional and confident, sharp (thinks on his feet and doesn't use canned speeches), honest (acknowledges potential shortcomings), and reflective (listens rather than tells)?

Just as salespeople are trying to qualify customers, so too are customers qualifying salespeople. Executives we have met with have revealed that they value dealing with salespeople who solved similar business problems for other customers. One executive said: "They understand that their solution may not be a panacea, and they deliver business value by helping me explore various options. My objective is to discuss and develop realistic solutions, not to see a slick sales presentation."

A CREDIBILITY GAP

While many of our interviews with executives focused on how salespeople need to engage more in terms of the Buyer's Journey and less in terms of an arbitrary sales cycle, selling is meaningless unless you can actually deliver the value you promise. We wondered how well most companies deliver the goods after the sale is made. One executive summed up her experience with the following anecdote:

> A man dies and finds himself at the Pearly Gates with both St. Peter and the devil. St. Peter says, "You're not supposed to die for another ten years. We'll have to send you back." The man is thrilled, but on his way out he sees one door to Heaven and another to Hell.
>
> He hears a raging party behind the door to Hell and asks the devil standing guard if he can take a peek. The devil says, "Only for a minute." So he goes through the door to Hell and finds an incredible party, with endless food, champagne, music, and every rock star from history beckoning him to join them. He says, "If this is Hell, I want in!"
>
> When he returns to Earth, he spends the next decade committing every sin he knows, and a few he had to look up on the Internet. Ten years to the day, he dies and meets the devil in front of the door to Hell. As the door opens, he hears no music and sees no party; only brimstone, fire, and the wailing of a thousand damned souls.
>
> He cries, "Wait! Where's the party?" The devil smiles and explains, "Oh, ten years ago you were a prospect. Now you're a customer."

As you can see, this story exemplifies how salespeople promise a lot to get the sale—but often don't deliver on those promises.

Accordingly, our research asked: "What benefits did you expect versus what was delivered from strategic suppliers?" The criteria that executives commented on are not as instructive as the startling differences between expectation and delivery in each case.

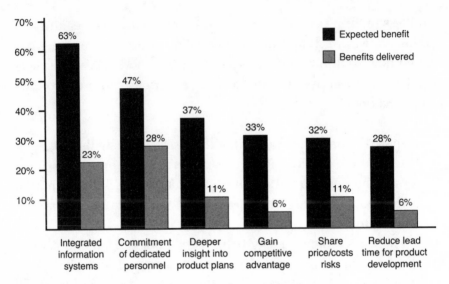

Figure 6.1 Expected Benefits vs. Benefits Delivered

As shown in Figure 6.1, most executives feel that they do not receive the expected benefits from strategic partners. Maybe the supplier failed in its delivery or the solution did not work as the executive hoped. Maybe the customer dropped the ball after taking delivery of the solution. Or perhaps the value was delivered and nobody closed the loop with the executive. Whatever the reasons, there is such a wide gap between the expected and realized benefits that it prompts the question, "What exactly do executives want from a sales organization?" One executive succinctly gave the answer as: "Integrity in the way a salesperson works with us, along with a track record of delivering on what was promised. Credibility is the product of those two."

All three studies reinforce this executive's interpretation (see Figure 6.2). According to the studies, building credibility comes from providing executives with a sense that you understand their business, you have the capability and experience to help them solve

CRITERIA	STUDY 1 USA 1995 Av. Score (1–5)	STUDY 2 USA 1999 Av. Score (1–5)	STUDY 3 ASIA 2005 Av. Score (1–5)
Ability to marshal resources	4.44	4.18	4.23
Understood my business goals	4.40	4.52	4.65
Responsiveness to my requests	4.36	4.56	4.62
Willingness to be held accountable	4.32	4.70	4.81
Knowledge of company's products	4.08	4.11	4.14
Demonstrated ability to solve problems	4.00	4.31	4.24
Works well with my staff	3.96	3.79	3.81
Knowledge of my industry	3.88	3.70	3.75
Knowledge of their own industry	3.76	4.34	4.44
Track record of accomplishments	3.60	3.93	3.70
Understands my personal issues	3.32	3.03	3.21
Source of information about competitors	2.84	2.70	2.81
Length of service in job	2.48	2.40	1.81

Figure 6.2 Executives' Expectations of Salespeople

their problems, and your intention is to establish lasting relationships and become their Trusted Advisor. Credibility is the result of the value that a salesperson or a sales organization brings to the executive over the long term.

A demonstrated ability to think beyond the current sales opportunity is also critical to the executive's perception of a salesperson's credibility. The sales organization must manage the relationship for the good of the customer, not simply from one sales opportunity to another.

Let's examine in some detail the top four criteria identified by executives as the key ingredients for building credibility with them (see Figure 6.2). What do they mean, and why are they important?

Ability to Marshal Resources

"Ability to marshal resources" was the single most important factor cited for building credibility in our original study. This represents a shift from the "lone wolf" salesperson toward building customer relationships involving multiple business functions. It also involves the formation of a virtual sales organization that is designed to bring the customer a total solution. Executives want comprehensive solutions that address their global business requirements. They also want a single point of contact within the sales organization who has responsibility and accountability for the solution.

This means that a single salesperson will not be able to go it alone. He may have to engage additional experts from within his own firm, coordinate across geographic boundaries, and work with a variety of business partners to help his customers solve complex business problems. Executives want to know that a single point of contact can represent them within the salesperson's own organization and has the ability to get things done. According to one executive, "If salespeople bring the right resources to us, avoiding the 'sales mode' by staying in an 'action and results' mode, it builds a lot of confidence." The ability of salespeople to wield influence within their own organizations and to bring the right resources to bear on their customers' needs are of prime importance here.

Understands Business Goals and Objectives

A critical way in which salespeople can successfully establish credibility is by having the ability to understand the customers' needs, including their goals and their key business drivers. Business drivers can be defined as the internal and external pressures that create the need for change. These pressures can create both problems and opportunities for the customer, with specific consequences and paybacks. The most pressing problems and opportunities subsequently result in distinct business initiatives. Without that understanding, there is no reference point that the salesperson can use to gauge the fit of a product or service. Focusing solely on the sale—with no context of how a solution benefits the customer's world—will create the view that the salesperson "is interested only in the commission."

Responsive to Requests

Executives want to do business with people who respond to their needs. They want to know that "when the salesperson says she's going to do something, she will deliver." In most organizations, the ability to be responsive involves the salesperson's ability to bring the appropriate resources to bear on the customers' requirements. Therefore, to build credibility, not only does the salesperson need to be personally responsive, but she needs to have enough influence to convince others within her own organization to be responsive as well. One executive cited a salesperson's ability to "tell me what she can do and make certain she also tells me what she can't do—both are important." This same executive went on to say that it is also important to "make certain that you can deliver on what you say you can do."

Willingness to Be Held Accountable

Executives realize that problems will occur at some point in time—that's a fact of business life. But how those problems are handled is the difference between establishing credibility or culpability. Executives want to minimize conversations with different people who are unfamiliar with their situation. They want one point of contact within an organization for problem resolution.

One executive stated, "I want the salesperson to take ownership of the problem, recognize that it exists, and secure the resources to solve it. I don't want the problem to be mine. That's one of the reasons why I worked with someone outside our organization in the first place."

Another executive took this point a step further by saying, "I look to people outside our organization to provide expertise that we don't have. We don't ask salespeople to do things we can do ourselves."

Knowing and understanding this, salespeople who provide business value to the customer will readily build credibility with customer executives.

Note that a salesperson's willingness to be held accountable rose to the number one rank in the second and third studies.

CLOSING THE CREDIBILITY GAP

Building credibility with senior-level customer executives is a critical factor in developing lasting business relationships. Becoming a Trusted Advisor to these executives should be a major objective of most salespeople involved in high-value, complex sales.

So, how is credibility developed over the long term? It comes about when the salesperson demonstrates both his capability and his integrity. Figure 6.3 depicts the two components of credibility, with "capability" on the x axis and "integrity" on the y axis. If you've already met with the relevant executive, that person will have made some initial assumptions about the potential value you could bring to her organization and perhaps even to her personally.

Salespeople who are seeking only a Problem Solver relationship will proceed only in the horizontal direction. It's clear that you must display your capability but be careful that you don't become seen as merely an "extra pair of hands" or an "expert for hire," as this can lead to your being engaged only on a transactional basis, where your relationship will be managed at the lower levels.

To enhance the relationship, you must continually demonstrate your integrity and your customer focus, which will ultimately build trust. Your objective in moving in this direction is to be perceived as reliable on a consistent basis—someone whom the executive receives increasing exposure to by virtue of the value you

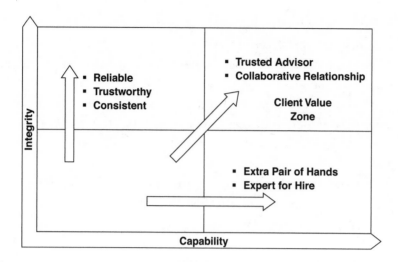

Figure 6.3 Components of Credibility

(Image adapted from Jagdish Shoth and Andrew Sobel, Clients for Life. New York: Simon & Schuster, 2000.)

start to add and get credit for. This is the hallmark of an Emerging Resource. But be careful that you don't build only the integrity of the relationship to the detriment of the capability aspect, or you might end up as the executive's best new friend who gets plenty of golfing dates but no sales!

To come to be perceived as a Trusted Advisor, you'll have to move up on both axes at the same time so that you can operate in the Client Value Zone. Here's where you'll come to be perceived as a Trusted Advisor and start to develop a collaborative relationship with the client executive. Trusted Advisors contribute to the client's success and view that success as critical to their own success.

You'll know you're in the Client Value Zone when the executive:

- Shares confidential information with you.
- Unveils his long-range plans to give you an advantage in preparing a response to his proposal.

- Asks you to come in at an early stage in his buying cycle to help establish the objectives of the project.
- Asks you for advice on issues that were unrelated to your company's solutions.
- Asks you to sit in on key strategic planning meetings or staff meetings, demonstrating that you are part of the client team.
- Values your success and demonstrates a keen interest in making you successful.
- Asks you to help him write a requirements definition for a new project—or even asks you to help him create an RFP, presentation, or other documents.
- Asks you to meet him at an off-site location so that he can reveal critical information to you.

This story from one of the authors further illustrates these points. When Steve managed an IBM division that sold technology to K–12 schools, the program arranged exclusive conferences for school leaders. Some of these lasted a whole week. A condition was the IBM salesperson had to escort the client and stick with them the whole time. One school superintendent enrolled from a prestigious school district, but the salesperson didn't want to take so much time away from their territory. Steve pointed out the client couldn't attend without the salesperson, and reluctantly the salesperson agreed to go. When the event was in session, Steve carefully observed the dynamic between salesperson and executive. It started slowly, but they developed a more robust dialogue each day. After the event, the salesperson thanked Steve for "forcing him to attend the session." It had drawn him much closer to his customer on a personal level, and he also significantly enhanced the business relationship. Later, this salesperson began to close significant business with this school district for many years, and claimed that much of that success was a result of the time they spent together.

This story illustrates a revision we suggest to the old adage, "People buy from people they like." While this may be a true saying, it's not entirely accurate when it comes to the way senior executives make buying decisions. Our research, as well as the experience of that IBM salesperson, clearly indicates that personal feelings are usually not the deciding factor. Instead, "people buy from people they trust" is a more accurate description. When you combine a business relationship with a personal, trust-based relationship, you increase your chances of being a Trusted Advisor.

"Say I've got a problem I need solved," says one executive. "I know two people who have expertise in that area. One of them I trust and respect. The other might actually have more expertise, but I don't know her as well. If I call the one I trust, I'll begin to act on his advice immediately. If I call the other one, I'll probably double-check and get a second opinion."

According to the executives, another essential factor in building trust is the salesperson's candor. Executives can sense when someone is not telling the whole story. Trust erodes quickly when an executive feels that the salesperson is not "coming clean." Executives stated that salespeople who misled them made them "wonder what other bombs may be waiting to explode." One executive realized that "there are challenges for all solutions to my business problems. I want to get as clear an indication as possible of what those are up front, warts and all."

Top-performing salespeople understand that building credibility at the executive level comes from providing the executive with a sense that they understand the business, they have the capability and experience to help the executive solve her business problems, and they intend to establish lasting relationships. In addition, executives want to know that they can count on you to represent them within your organization. This enables the salesperson to enhance the relationship and become the executive's Trusted Advisor. A salesperson's objective should be to move toward the upper right, in the direction of the Client Value Zone, as depicted in Figure 6.3.

Here's what one sales professional shared about this topic:

My customer was number three in the check printing business, and volume had been increasing dramatically. Flush with funds, the CEO saw a window of opportunity to improve the company's manufacturing process and get ahead of its competitors. But most employees didn't see this vision and were content to increase capacity in an incremental fashion. Bidding for that work would have done little to help the customer and would have been low value for us. I undertook an in-depth study of the company's manufacturing process and asked the CEO who was the best person to show me how it really worked. He introduced me to a manufacturing worker who was not a decision maker but who was clearly trusted by the CEO. In fact he'd been challenged to develop new solutions in the manufacturing process. I agreed to spend time with him, with the proviso that I could return to the CEO to report our findings.

The outcome of the study was a recommendation for a unique process-control computer that could manage the check printing process to increase throughput by a factor of 20. The ROI was less than 12 months, and the solution would provide substantial growth over the next 10 years. During my presentation, the CEO kept nodding positively, then turned to his CFO and asked, "Do you see any reason why we shouldn't do this?" A year later after the new computer system was installed, the firm was number two in the market.

Remember, building credibility with executives by demonstrating both your technical or delivery capability and your personal integrity and customer focus is based almost entirely on your ability to both understand and interpret the executive's business drivers, as outlined earlier in the section in Chapter 3 titled "The Drivers of Executive Decision Making." You must frame your value in the context of your customers' world.

HOW TO MAKE AN IMPRESSION ON AN EXECUTIVE

It's obvious that salespeople cannot simply go in there and "wing it." Let's explore how you need to conduct yourself and what impression you need to leave (see Figure 6.4).

CRITERIA	STUDY 1 USA 1995 Av. Score (1–5)	STUDY 2 USA 1999 Av. Score (1–5)	STUDY 3 ASIA 2005 Av. Score (1–5)
Demonstrated accountability	4.48	4.49	4.37
Understood my business goals	4.40	4.59	4.45
Listened before prescribing	4.36	4.59	4.71
Knowledge of industry/company	4.36	4.02	4.81
Had a game plan for next steps	4.20	3.79	4.14
Ability to solve problems	4.00	4.15	4.31
The meeting achieved stated objectives	4.00	3.79	3.52
Communicated value	3.96	3.95	4.59
Proposed alternative solutions	3.88	3.69	2.95
Thinking beyond the current sale	3.84	3.56	4.11
Works well with my staff	3.76	3.77	3.88
Prepared and followed a meeting agenda	3.48	3.52	4.20
Source of information about competitors	2.72	2.95	4.36

Figure 6.4 The First Meeting with a Senior Executive

Demonstrated Accountability

Executives confirmed that they expect the buck to start and stop with you. They look for salespeople who are willing to be held accountable for both the success *and* the failure of their organization's ability to provide service and drive results. It turns an executive off when she hears a salesperson say that he cannot do something because he lacks the authority or control. When this happens, the sales rep is admitting to being roadkill, and the executive will see the vultures circling overhead and disengage from the Empty Suit Salesperson. Demonstrating accountability means taking the lumps and not hiding when things go wrong (and having a plan to resolve the problems), being the single point of contact, and showing that a method for measuring your contribution exists. Executives don't want you to represent your company to them as much as they want you to represent them to your company and to be their agent on the inside who knows her way around the organization and can tap into the pockets of value to make a difference.

The executives we tested in China told us that they don't look for accountability from an individual salesperson. Instead, they expect the salesperson to elevate them, brokering a relationship with a peer in the vendor organization so that they can speak with an equal. In a market in which annual attrition of salespeople is 62 percent, executives expect salespeople to open the door, but don't expect them to stick around long enough to be accountable for anything.[1] This is another reason they crave peer relationships, as well as for *guanxi*. We expect that as Asian markets mature and people stay in roles longer, this criterion may adjust so that it is in line with what we see in other developed nations. For example, in 2017 salesperson attrition is 27 percent in the United States—which is half the rate in China yet still twice the national average in the overall labor force.[2]

Understood My Business Goals

In the five years between the first and second research studies, a subtle shift occurred. Executives started rating "understood my business goals" and "listened before prescribing a solution" higher than the previously more popular "demonstrated accountability." The change indicates that in a period of dot-com excess, budgets under scrutiny, and high stakes, executives wanted to know that the decisions they were making were backed by sound analysis and due diligence.

Together, these top three criteria remain critical and were only made more relevant by the scandals involving Enron and Arthur Andersen, Bernie Madoff, WorldCom, Barings Bank and Nick Leeson, Lloyds of London, Harshad Mehta of India, Parmalat of Italy, the Metallgesellschaft affair in Germany, Daiwa Bank and Toshihide Iguchi in Japan, the HIH Insurance collapse in Australia, Wells Fargo's massive opening of fraudulent accounts, Volkswagen's emission scandal, Toshiba's accounting issues and others, and the subsequent tightening of controls. More than ever, executives like to have an audit trail for their decision-making process and to know that investments are not being made on a whim or out of cronyism. Salespeople who provide a structured approach, from discovery to recommendation, are welcome standouts.

Listened Before Prescribing a Solution

This goes hand in hand with "understood my business goals." Make certain you develop a questioning strategy in advance of any call on a senior executive. While doing your research, develop a list of *consultative-type questions* that you could pose that are clearly aligned with the executive's business goals and objectives. Use those questions to probe further so that you leave an impression on the executive that you are not there for a quick sale, that you have carefully done your homework, and that you plan to represent their interests and serve as their spokesperson within your company.

A few well-selected questions, then a willing ear, make for some of the best sales calls you will ever participate in. Let the executive talk! A sales director in Finland believes, "When you are talking, you hear only what you already know. When you are listening, you hear what you need to know!"

Salespeople who take this approach are sometimes bewildered by the results. Said one, "I really didn't do that much. I asked a few simple questions. The customer provided the answers. Then I read back a summary of what he'd said. On hearing his own words, he gave me the credit for being a great consultant with all the answers."

Doctors who get a reputation for having all the answers begin by teasing those answers out of the patient's head and letting them find expression. Most executives know what they need, especially those who have already done their homework using the Internet and other public sources of information. What they lack is time: time to reflect and time to find direction. So give them that time, and be courageous in the moments of silence. Silence is golden because it is when thoughts find their structure. Let it happen, and avoid the primal urge to fill an uncomfortable silence with your own patter.

Listening is incomplete until it is joined with *prescribing* a solution. So when you have all the executive's ideas, pains, concerns, and shopping lists on the table, this is where you add your own expertise in weaving together a debriefing on where her ideas are sound, where they could be improved, and what a working solution using your products, services, and resources would look like. This is where having done your homework will absolutely serve you well. The executive wants certainty, and she will buy from people who show confidence in a solution that the executive can see her own thumbprint on. Knowing her key business issues and her key business objectives will help guide you toward a solution that she feels she helped to create.

Knowledge of Industry/Company

Executives invest time with salespeople who provide insight. The best way to deliver that insight is to think of the first meeting as a job interview, as mentioned earlier, and to promote yourself as the sort of person who would make an immediate impact if the executive hired you for his team. To do this, you need to be up to date on the events of both your industry and his, and to know how his business works. You will find a guide on how to find this information in Appendix A.

Once you have this knowledge, life becomes much easier. You can treat the first meeting and those that follow as mini-board meetings where you speak with the executive as a peer, talking not about the generic features of your product, but about the specific outcome it can drive in the business and your road map for how to get there.

Executives explained that they expect incumbent suppliers to use their knowledge of both companies to drive efficiencies. One said:

> When we bring on a supplier, we know it will take a few months for the supplier's representative to settle in and learn how we do things. After that orientation, I judge good suppliers as the ones whose representatives say things like, "We've been looking at how you do this or that around here, and we think there's a better way." When she serves as a fresh pair of eyes and uses her knowledge about my company to make suggestions nobody else has, it guarantees the longevity of the relationship. She also needs to know her own industry developments to ensure that she's giving me the most up-to-date feedback. There's nothing less valuable than yesterday's newspaper.

"Knowledge of industry/company" ranked highest of all criteria in our China study. Why is this the most important trait to China's executives? It has to do with the unique evolution of China since its 2001 entry into the World Trade Organization.

Western countries saw their infrastructures, technology, pop culture, brands, and business processes evolve in stages over the past 30 years. We all moved at a similar pace as some ways of working died out and new ones took their place. For example, 40 years ago, it was common for companies to have a typing pool of secretaries, bulky steel typewriters, messy carbon ribbons, and central filing of each original. Whole paper-based industries and brands rose up to support this way of working. Today, executives type their own e-mails, and so the secretarial typing pool, typewriters, and carbon ribbons are all but gone in the West. This shift to personal production drove a work culture of greater personal empowerment to get things done.

But in China, the typing pools of secretaries and central filing of carefully stamped or "chopped" triplicates are still commonplace alongside modern laser printers and blade servers. As in some science fiction tale, three decades of technology and business process overlap in the same space-time continuum. It's not unusual to experience massive confusion—and therefore slow decision making—as Chinese executives face a cornucopia of bewildering options, all of them touted as the "latest and greatest." These executives admit that they don't always know whether they're investing in something new or in something that the West dispensed with 15 years ago—to them, it *all* looks new.

In such a situation, we can better appreciate why they so highly rate the ability of a salesperson (or the salesperson's manager) to bring knowledge of the industry to help them make sense of their many options and reduce the risk of losing face as a result of a wrong decision. Is this really so different from the needs of Western executives?

Your objective in developing knowledge about your client's industry, as well as their company, is simple: You want to develop insights about your client's industry that impact your client's company—insights the client executive may be unaware of which can help them achieve their objectives.

An example can be found in the novel *Gone Girl*, by Gillian Flynn (Crown Publishing Group, 2012). When Nick Dunne meets his controversial attorney for the first time, Tanner Bolt says: "I try never to show up at one of these meetings without new information for my client. I want to show you how serious I am about your case—and how much you need me!"

That's exactly what you are trying to do—provide the client executive with some new information or insight they may be unaware of, or at least help them see old information through a new lens that grants them unexpected perspective.

Ability to Solve Problems

When salespeople read this criterion, they conclude that the operative word is *solve*. Those of us in sales and marketing have an obsession with *solutions*. Type the words *your* and *solutions* into Google and insert any word in between, and you will quickly see that solutions exist for everything you need in life:

- Birth solutions
- Education solutions
- Dating solutions
- Wedding solutions
- Pregnancy solutions
- Parenting solutions
- Career solutions
- Real estate solutions
- Wealth solutions
- Vacation solutions
- Retirement solutions

And in a recent walk through New York City, the number of taxicabs and buses advertising everything from toenail solutions and credit solutions to hair solutions and get-rich-quick solutions couldn't be counted. The world has gone solution-crazy, affixing the word to situations that have nothing to do with problems at all. People say *solution* when they mean *product*. So many salespeople now wax lyrical about the *synergy* of their *value-added, collaborative, enterprise-wide world-class solution* that such words have become meaningless.

With all this white noise, what is a real solution? The word *solution* originates in the discipline of chemistry, where a solution is described as "a mixture comprising one or more solutes that are dissolved by a solvent of greater volume." A packet of Kool-Aid crystals (the solute) makes a refreshing beverage when the crystals are dissolved in a greater volume of water (the solvent). When your client has a defined business problem (the solute), your job is to dissolve it by application of your product or service (the solvent). This is the proper application of terms like *solve* and *solution*—they are meaningless outside of the context of a problem.

This is why the focus in the phrase "ability to solve problems" is not on the word *solve* but on the word *problem*. Without a problem, there can be no solution. Executives told us that the criteria "understood my business goals," "listened before prescribing," and "knowledge of industry/company" are all essential if salespeople are to gain a comprehensive picture of the executive's world and its unique challenges and problems. Only then do executives believe that a salesperson has the "ability to solve problems."

Tips for understanding the executive's problems were given in the first three chapters of this book. Appendix A provides other ideas that you can immediately apply.

Communicated Value

People at the operations level are focused on "What does your product do?" (features, functions, and their application).

People in middle management are more interested in "How will it fit into the operation?" (nonproduct issues such as total cost of ownership, implementation, training, and the impact on other processes).

At the executive level, the question changes to "Why should we do this at all?" Executives know that a dollar spent in one area is a dollar that cannot be spent in another area. So they want to know, "Do we spend $5 million on upgrading our information systems, or do we invest $5 million in a new manufacturing plant in Eastern Europe? Should we invest it in a new ad campaign, or should we build our staff an indoor squash court?" Sometimes your biggest competitor can actually be the alternative ways in which a customer's capital can be spent and the competing priorities to do so.

As Figure 6.5 illustrates, the importance of communicating value at the executive level is that, from the executive's vantage point, he has a companywide mandate to effect change, and he can tap into funds across the company to carry out his goals. When you sell to executives, the time it takes to go from spiel to deal is often shorter, but you must frame all your discussion around why this project is the right horse to back, and what the value of doing so will be.

Executives in China gave this issue of communicating value the third highest rating, compared to a rank of sixth in the US studies.

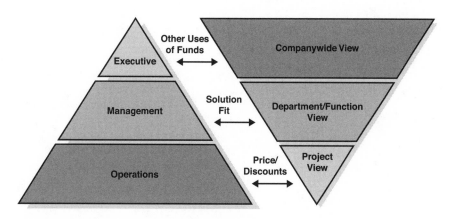

Figure 6.5 Different Stakeholders' Perspectives

In China, the subtext is, "How will this decision make me look? Can I leverage it for greater *guanxi*?" Chinese executives test to know whether the salesperson can become an extension of their personal network and bring them value. When you think it through, that's no different to executives anywhere else.

CHAPTER SUMMARY

Let's summarize what we've discussed in this chapter about the third question in our research: "How can salespeople establish credibility with executives?" Let's break it down to the top four messages:

1. *Know their expectations.* Executives expect the salespeople they deal with to exhibit general qualities that make them stand out in a sea of look-alikes. They expect you to be able to understand their business goals, marshal your company's resources, be responsive to the executive's requests, and be accountable when things go wrong. They also expect you to listen before you prescribe a solution, to do so in the context of the executive's company and industry, to solve problems when they arise, and to return to communicate the value delivered. Beyond these general expectations are the specific expectations for the project they engage you for. But clearly their priority is on you as a person. As one executive told us: "Get people with the right values and behaviors on the team and business will work itself out."

2. *Always exceed their expectations.* Executives feel that suppliers generally don't deliver what they say they will. They are unimpressed by salespeople who pitch canned rhetoric that fails to connect with their issues. They don't need talking brochures, with the word *solution* applied in all the wrong places. They use a first meeting to filter salespeople who had the ability to get through the door from salespeople who will be invited back again. Salespeople who show the right capabilities gain credibility and continued access. You get only one chance to make a good first impression.

3. *Operate in the Client Value Zone.* People buy from people they like, and they are always looking for Emerging Resources to begin to make a contribution to their organization. People also buy from people they trust, and they are always looking for Problem Solvers to clearly make a difference. At the lowest level, Commodity Suppliers are those who simply turn up to make a sale, and these almost never rate a meeting with an executive. At the highest level, Trusted Advisors are those who build trust and demonstrate their capability in equal measure. They move past the rest and become part of the executive's circle of advisors. This is what you need to aim at if your goal is to consistently sell at the executive level.

4. *Prepare, prepare, prepare.* Develop a questioning strategy in advance of your call on a customer executive. Make certain the executive understands that you have done your homework and understand their business goals and objectives. Come to the meeting with information and insights the executive may not be aware of, so that you can demonstrate your continued value to the company, as well as to the executive. Remember, executives don't expect to educate you, they expect you to be prepared for your meeting with them. Lastly, executives buy not when they understand, but when they feel they are understood. Listen carefully before proposing your solution.

Chapter 7

How to Create Value for the C-Suite

Executives believe that meetings are a forum for exchanging ideas, and they are prepared to be led by a skilled questioner along a path of discovery in the hope that the salesperson knows what he needs to find out from the executive in order to make appropriate recommendations. Salespeople who ask the right questions to uncover problems impress senior executives.

Salespeople with experience selling to operations and middle management personnel must therefore modify their approach at the executive level. Those who give a boilerplate presentation on why their product is the best are unlikely to make progress. A number of executives told us that they feel that these canned speeches mean, "The salesperson has a pitch she wants to deliver rather than listening to my concerns." Others said: "There are a lot of salespeople who say they have the answer before they know what the problem is."

One executive said: "If I have to ask the questions or uncover all the problems, the rep is of no use to me. I look for people who ask layers of questions that uncover something I might not have considered." Note the term *layers of questions*. Executives don't want us to ask questions that merely skim the surface on the way to our product pitch. They expect a meaningful, deliberate interview that digs deep into the well of their discontent until they have unburdened themselves, arrived at the root causes, and have the potential cures before them. Salespeople who follow a structured questioning framework to bring a new perspective to an existing situation will always provide value.

This means that the majority of the meeting should be spent on understanding the problems, issues, and implications associated with the opportunity or situation. The key is to listen, ask questions, and let the executive reveal the problems and the impact that these problems are having on the organization.

STRUCTURING MEETINGS WITH THE EXECUTIVE

There is a template in Appendix B (see "Executive-Level Meeting Planner") that you can use to help you structure your face-to-face meetings with executives to discuss their needs. Structuring an initial meeting with executives follows the same format as the pie chart in Figure 7.1, which suggests that your meeting should have an *introduction*, followed by a discussion of *issues and implications*, then deal with *solution options*, and end with *moving forward*.

The pie chart in Figure 7.1 also suggests the relative amount of time that executives told us they feel should be devoted to each part of the meeting.

For example, if the pie chart were for a one-hour meeting, the introduction might take 10 minutes, issues and implications might take 25 minutes, solution options might take 15 minutes, and agreeing on the steps for moving forward might take another 10 minutes.

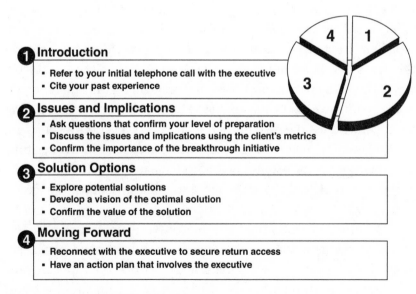

① Introduction
- Refer to your initial telephone call with the executive
- Cite your past experience

② Issues and Implications
- Ask questions that confirm your level of preparation
- Discuss the issues and implications using the client's metrics
- Confirm the importance of the breakthrough initiative

③ Solution Options
- Explore potential solutions
- Develop a vision of the optimal solution
- Confirm the value of the solution

④ Moving Forward
- Reconnect with the executive to secure return access
- Have an action plan that involves the executive

Figure 7.1 Structuring the First Meeting

1. Introduction

In the introduction stage of the meeting, you should refer to the initial phone call you made to the executive, citing your sponsor or referrer if appropriate. Give the executive a glimpse of some of your past experience, either in his organization or with similar clients. Set an expectation for the mutual value you expect the meeting to deliver. Meetings without a stated outcome are usually a waste of an executive's time.

2. Issues and Implications

This is the area you'll spend most of your time on during the first meeting. Ask questions that get you credit for having done your homework. Listen intently, and discuss the client's key business issues, using their metrics. Develop an understanding of this executive's breakthrough initiative and its importance at a personal and company level. The breakthrough initiative is the most important initiative that the client must act upon. It is typically bound by a time frame and accompanied by either significant payback if implemented or consequences if not acted upon. And in many cases, the breakthrough initiative is developed at the executive level and often not even recognized or even known at lower levels of the client organization. If your solution addresses and can provide value for this breakthrough initiative, you will get the executive's attention. However, it's a good idea to leave questions related to solution options for later in the meeting. Once you move to those questions, it's often hard for both you and the client to step back to the broader, more strategic questions. Try these:

- "What effect has this problem had on your organization?" Use the knowledge gained from your research to expand on the situation. This question helps the executive focus on a specific area of the business and allows you to showcase your knowledge of the organization and its industry.

- "What three things are you not doing today that would help you resolve the problem? Which one of these is most important to you and why?" These questions will help you understand the gap between what the company is currently doing and what the executive feels it should be doing. More importantly, the answer to the second question will help you focus better on the area most important to the executive. Your goal is to pose such a series of questions to a senior executive and have them step back and go "Wow! Where did you get those questions from? They're really making me think!"
- "What have you done to address this problem? Why did you choose this solution? What was the outcome?" These questions all focus on using the past to understand the executive's thought process.
- "What do you see as the critical success factors for solving this problem?" This question uncovers whether the executive knows what she wants to do and gives clues about how she will measure the success of the project.
- "What are the consequences if you don't solve the problem?" This question uncovers whether this problem or situation has a compelling event that will cause pain if it is not solved within a certain time frame. If the situation has no compelling event, then pursuing a solution might not be worth the time and resources it will require.
- "Who are the key people I should talk to in your organization to better understand the problem?" With this question, you're volunteering to be sent down to lower levels in the organization to develop a better understanding of the next steps, thus allowing the executive to view you as a resource.

As you are posing these types of questions, make certain you are asking them using the client's metrics and terminology. This will strengthen your ability to appear as an industry insider and improve your credibility with the executive.

3. Solution Options

Only *after* the issue has been clearly defined and agreed upon should a salesperson begin to describe potential solutions that can be related to business value. Waiting until the end of the meeting to explore solutions builds credibility with the executive. Keep your product in your pocket until it's time to bring it out.

Discuss potential solutions and their value to both the company at a business level *and* the executive at a personal level. Develop the executive's vision of the optimal solution. What ideas has he already entertained? Watch for the executive's passion as he describes this vision! Don't necessarily reveal *your* company's solution at this point, simply confirm the executive's perception of what value looks like to him.

4. Moving Forward

Find a way to get the executive involved in a follow-on meeting to explore these issues in more detail. For the later meeting, you would plan to return with an expert such as a solution manager or some other presales resource to take the discussion to the next level. The executive might send you down to meet with a lower-level executive. This is not always a bad thing if you ask her to make the introduction for you, and if she agrees to reconnect with you after that meeting to review your findings. Being able to legitimately say, "The boss sent me," is like having a skeleton key that will open most doors.

Executives told us that they don't appreciate salespeople who script their meeting agenda so tightly that there's no room for creative discussion. This occurs when the rep is given a one-hour meeting block and packs enough slides to fill the whole hour. In such a setting, 20 minutes or less of presentation and 40 minutes or more of discussion is a better ratio. At its most ridiculous, we've seen this dogmatic approach lead to the executive saying, "I'm convinced; where do I sign?" and the salesperson selling beyond the close with words to the effect: "Let me just explain the benefits." Don't laugh—you'd be surprised how often we see this. Whatever sales school these salespeople went to, they learned a prescriptive approach that doesn't fit the C-Suite.

As we outlined earlier, product-focused Commodity Suppliers are living in a world that doesn't really exist anymore. As a technically oriented Emerging Resource, you're living dangerously close to that old world. As a value-driven Problem Solver or Trusted Advisor who is prepared to have a robust discussion, you're at home in the new world of selling.

There was once a printing company that was expanding its business to include production of its own line of greeting cards, which it intended to distribute through retail outlets, a market the company had never sold through before.

The executive in charge asked all potential suppliers to bring him ideas on the most efficient ways to procure paper and cards for what the company anticipated would be a business with seasonal peaks.

One supplier presented several innovative suggestions about just-in-time delivery and even provided a helpful market assessment of other greeting card businesses that included the most popular card stock, sizes, and designs. The executive wanted to buy from this supplier, but his budget was not high enough, and with regret he gave a $500,000 order to a Commodity Supplier whose prices had been assessed over the Internet as being the best for cash flow.

After sending the purchase order, the paper executive called the sales manager at the winning vendor and asked whether the salesperson would receive a commission on the sale.

"Of course," was the reply.

"How much?" asked the client.

"Fifteen percent of the total sale," was the eventual answer.

The executive did some mental arithmetic. "Good," he said to the client. "Then I want my invoice reduced by $75,000 because your salesperson sold us nothing at all."

He won his concession, and he diverted the savings into a bonus for the salesperson from the other supplier who had contributed so many good ideas!

If you're a Problem Solver to your client, you see the client as a business peer because you view her business through the same lens as the relevant executive, not through the lens of a salesperson looking for a need to sell to. By researching the business using the tools we've discussed, preparing the approach, building support with influential stakeholders, and asking high-yield questions, every salesperson can sell effectively at the executive level.

Let's now discuss the concept of the value propositions we must all eventually present to our executive buyers.

GOING ONCE, TWICE, THREE TIMES—SOLD!

In the life cycle of a client, there are three times when you should sell your value.

1. Value Hypothesis

When you're on the outside hoping to gain an audience and make your first sale into an account, you should use your research to determine whether the account can *probably* derive some benefit from what you sell. You don't really know for sure. And without a discussion in which the customer validates your assumptions and provides real data, all you have is a *value hypothesis*, a guess and a hope of things that might be. Like a coloring book page, you can see an outline, but it holds no tone or definition. Value hypotheses are what marketing departments send out when they're troubling a customer about his problems—a glimpse of a desired future state.

At the very minimum, salespeople should customize these documents and tailor them to the specific client opportunity.

2. Value Proposition

When you're talking to a qualified prospect and she's explaining the *how much, how often,* and *who to* aspects of the problems she faces (or the opportunities she wants to leverage), you are getting closer to knowing what the basis of your *value proposition* is going to be. It's impossible to write a value proposition unless you know what to propose, and to get at this information, you must convince the prospect to disclose something about how her business operates, where the dysfunction and costs reside, and what her vision is for an alternative. You then map your capabilities onto her requirements and return to the prospect with a specific plan that proposes a way for her to solve her problem or achieve her vision by using your capabilities. A good value proposition will always include measurements that explain:

> You want to do Z, which we can deliver at a cost of Y. This will reduce current costs by X and improve efficiency by W, which over the space of V months with U people using it, will enable you to recoup your initial cost within T months and lift overall productivity by S, adding R to your bottom line in the first year. We have these capabilities, and we propose that if you start next month, we can have this process underway as fast as Q. By doing this, Department A will solve Issue B, which is of concern to Executive C. Stakeholder Group D will also benefit by having better access to E and F, saving G amounts of time that it can better devote to the task of H. By announcing this approach in your next press meeting, your CFO expects to lift your share price by J percent, which will raise your borrowing status to AAA and open up sources of capital to underwrite your expansion plans in Country K.

What you see in this alphabet soup is a value proposition that goes to the extent of naming specific people doing specific tasks, identifying how each will benefit, and determining the downstream impact on issues that you know are under discussion and are topical at the executive level. With this style of content, you're really *proposing* something. You're making an offer and packaging it in a compelling way.

The word *proposition* has a dictionary definition as follows:

An idea, offer, or plan put forward for consideration or discussion; a statement of opinion or judgment; a statement or theorem to be demonstrated.[1]

Executives told us that while millions of proposals are sent around the world each year, few of them actually *propose* anything. Don't get us wrong—most of these documents include a section dutifully titled "Value Proposition." But that's where the similarities to an actual proposition often end. There are few examples executives could recall where they sat back, rubbed their chin, and said, "Wow, I really love what these guys are proposing!" Instead of striking gold, they find their pans full of iron pyrite—fool's gold—as they read page after page of price lists and capability statements at the basic end of the spectrum, and overly detailed spreadsheets at the complex end. In few cases do they see anything that *tells a personalized story* with the names of their key stakeholders and the jobs they do, the challenges they face, and the goals they own, described against an overview of how each of these tasks and goals will be affected by a new solution. And yet, this is what executives want to see presented to them. They want suppliers to be specific and say, "This is how you do it today, this is why that isn't optimal, and we propose that if you do it our way, you'll get a specific result that looks like this."

The reason executives see winning value propositions like this all too rarely is because so many salespeople experience performance anxiety in the C-Suite; they don't relax enough, or they are so intent on getting their message across that they forget to ask the very questions they need the answers to if they are to be in a position to frame a value proposition later. In the absence of customer input, all a salesperson can present or write is the chaff that is putting executives to sleep.

When you are writing a winning value proposition, it pays to connect your customer's needs with the full range of your capabilities. Salespeople sometimes overlook some of their capabilities, and so those capabilities go unannounced and unappreciated.

For example, part of your value might be that you are able to bring some of the following elements to the table, in the knowledge that they are relevant to the customer:

- Products (proprietary or custom)
- Services and support capabilities
- The stability of your company as a supplier
- Knowledge of the problem
- Familiarity with the client's environment
- Your knowledge of what works and what doesn't
- Rapport with the client's people
- Expertise in solving this problem for others
- Specialist resources in your solution team
- Introductions to others in your network
- The value of business partners in making a solution complete
- The time you will save the client
- The costs (not just the price) you will save the client
- The added capability you will provide

Don't sell yourself short. There are always many elements of value that, as you sell every day, may have become things that you regard as self-evident and somewhat pedestrian to talk about. But to a customer who is buying your solutions intermittently or for the first time, what you see as commonplace may be a revelation.

If you don't spell it out for your customer, nobody will. As one sales director once said: "If you don't blow your own horn, your competition will use it as a spittoon!"

Just remember: Value is relevant only when it is explained in the context of its impact on specific problems or projects that a client has. If your value is not anchored in the client's problems, it will sound like a hustle.

Your differentiated value proposition begins with identifying your three components of value, as shown in Figure 7.2. Most salespeople only focus on the value of their company's solutions (the third component of value). When focusing only on this element, your solution can easily become commoditized. However, if you can clearly articulate your three components of value you will have started to develop a differentiated value proposition that can't be duplicated by your competitors. Let's take a look at the three components of value and review them in more detail.

- *Your personal value*—This element of value is often overlooked. Experienced salespeople gain knowledge of the client's industry and company. As outsiders looking in, and being able to

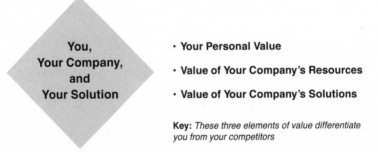

Figure 7.2 Your Three Components of Value

compare what they see in one company with techniques used in others, they can contribute significant value. When a salesperson is proficient at acquiring that type of knowledge, their ability to anticipate client requirements and deliver fresh ideas and insights is high—and client executives respect that. This trait ultimately enables you to be seen as a resource to the executive. As your ideas provide insight that even people within the executive's own organization can't provide, your stock rises.

One executive shared a story about a salesperson named Brad, who consistently achieved Trusted Advisor status. They would call to ask Brad's advice on issues that were totally unrelated to the information technology he sold. This vice president of manufacturing once asked Brad where to construct a new manufacturing plant to accommodate his company's rapid growth. The reason she did this was because she knew Brad had a thorough understanding of her company's business issues, the dynamics of their industry, and the geography of his territory. His ability to connect these dots surpassed that of people employed inside the client organization who rarely saw beyond their cubicle wall. When you take inventory of the personal knowledge and experience you bring to the table, you may be surprised by how valuable you are as a resource in your own right.

- *Your company's resources*—Typically, the salesperson's company has a multitude of resources that can potentially deliver value to the client. In many cases, these resources can be of significant value, so salespeople need to make certain that they get credit for this component. When attempting to quantify the value of your company's resources, don't overlook your product or service specialists or presales personnel, whom you could identify as part of this element of your value. Also remember to include items such as freemiums your company offers, or low-cost education, events, warranties, magazines and newsletters, access to support centers, and other resources that ring the client's bell. You may see these items so often they've stopped being wondrous in your eyes. Not so to someone seeing them for the first time!

- *Your company's solutions*—There's a danger this element of value is thought of as being all about the product's features and benefits. Certainly executives report it's the most emphasized when salespeople present to them. Yet your company's solution takes on a different dimension when expressed in terms of "hard" value and "soft" value. The hard value is about time or financial savings or gains from using the new product or service, compared to maintaining the status quo or buying a rival's solution. The soft value is more about the wow factor people will experience when they use your solution. This understanding doesn't come from a brochure. You can only learn how each type of user will benefit after you spend time to see how the tasks or operations are being performed today (prior to the implementation of your solution). You then project what will change in the before and after picture. Some of this relates back to time and money, but other aspects include considerations like frustration being replaced by ease and satisfaction, or risk and doubt being replaced by certainty and confidence. You may not be able to put a financial value on everything, and you don't need to. The executive will place his own value on them. Just make sure you list them and get the client to agree they're relevant and unique.

Taken together, these three elements of value uniquely differentiate you from your competitors. No other competitor can offer the same combination. This means no client can justify the purchasing department's typical gambit of commoditizing its suppliers, saying you all look alike, and declaring the best price wins. You elevate yourself above that fray when value is properly established.

It's critical that you view the creation of your value proposition from the client's perspective. Perhaps your solution addresses their breakthrough initiative, helps them take advantage of a limited window of opportunity, or resolves a problem that's causing customer complaints. If so, tell them. Put yourself in their shoes, then show that you see the opportunity from their perspective, share their concerns, but have some answers. Only then can they truly see how your personal integrity, experience, and knowledge (personal value), plus your company's other people, research, investments, resources, and know-how (company value), plus your actual products and services (solution value) come together in a way they can harness for their benefit.

When you overlay these three elements of value over the client's key business initiative, the intersection defines your specific business value (see Figure 7.3).

Your customer-focused value proposition will then answer three questions:

1. *What's important to the client?* Simply stated, a value proposition addresses the client's issues and focuses on a return on investment for his breakthrough initiative.
2. *How can we create value for the client?* Address this question by describing how *you, your company,* and *your solution* can help in both a qualitative and a quantitative way.

Figure 7.3 The Value Nexus

3. *How can we demonstrate our capability?* At the nexus between your solution and the client's breakthrough initiative is a working hypothesis of *your specific business value* in terms of how tasks will be performed using your solution and how outputs will be different (see Figure 7.3). Make certain that you paint a vivid picture of this specific business value.

We've established that you can construct a meaningful, customer-focused value proposition only if you have an understanding of the following:

- The customer's business initiative
- How your solution affects the business initiative
- What the customer's critical measurements are before your solution
- What the customer's measurements will be after your solution is in place
- The time frame for breakeven and ROI
- The three components of value (personal, company, solution)

Figure 7.4 provides a template you can use to construct a customer-focused value proposition for your client.

Demonstrating your capability can be as simple as providing an example of where you have delivered a similar solution before and the results you achieved as a result of implementing that solution. A template for that content is shown in Figure 7.5.

You should be capable of ____________________ by ____________________
(describe the impact) (monetary units or %)

through the ability to ____ .
(describe the new situation)

This will require an investment of ________________________________ ,
(state the cost of the solution)

which will be returned within ________________________________ .
(estimate the time frame for return)

Figure 7.4 Customer-Focused Value Proposition Template

You can add a credible reference to your Value Proposition with one additional sentence.

We recently implemented a similar solution at

________________________, who achieved ________________________ .
(name of client) (specific savings achieved)

Figure 7.5 Template for Adding a Reference

Developing a Customer-Focused Value Proposition

Let's say that your customer is experiencing problems with their service department. It currently has an interactive voice response telephone system that processes support requests from customers whose equipment has broken down.

Customers lodge their requests for repair, spare parts, or service via the phone, and these requests are automatically routed to a fleet of service vans using a global positioning system, based on which van is closest to the customer.

Recently, some jobs have been sent to more than one van, causing two or sometimes three service representatives to arrive at the same job. This diverts them from other work that could be billed and is a waste of time for everyone. It also creates conflict as they argue over who gets credit for turning up to the job, which has led to duplicate payments being made, which kills all profit from such jobs.

In this case, a good introduction to the value proposition would include a reference to this situation, as seen in Figure 7.6.

When your service vans are dispatched to customer sites, more than one van is sent to the same site on average 30 times per month per person across a service team of 150 people. This costs your service representatives 30 minutes on each occasion and, according to your CFO, $20,000 per year in extra fuel costs. We calculate the combined cost of fuel, unproductive time, and missed revenue from this problem is $850,000 per year.

Figure 7.6 Sample Value Proposition (Introduction)

Now that you have the customer's "before" picture set, you are ready to explain the "after" picture. Figure 7.7 shows a sample value proposition for this example; a copy of the template used to prepare it is also provided in Appendix B.

> You will **reduce instances of duplicated customer service visits** by **20%**, resulting in a **monthly saving of $250,000** by implementing our **Call Tracker system**. This will require an investment of **$2 million**, which will be returned in 8 months based on your figures of current occurences of the problem.
>
> We implemented a similar solution at **Acme Transfer Company**, who achieved a monthly saving of **$500,000 within 90 days** of installation.

Figure 7.7 Customer-Focused Value Proposition Example: Service Industry

Let's look at another example, only this time your customer is in healthcare, experiencing problems throughout their hospital system and in their surgical centers in particular. There are two specific concerns: an increase in surgical episode times and infections in the hospitals. Your company is a major provider of medical technology that addresses both issues.

After working with the relevant executive, the Chief Medical Officer (CMO), you have developed the customer-focused value proposition shown in Figure 7.8.

> You should be capable of **improving efficiencies and optimizing outcomes** through the use of **our new joint replacement techniques** and far exceed the **patient outcomes** you have achieved with your existing protocols.
>
> Our precision solutions are designed to create a **reduction in surgical episode time**, which can lead to an increased number of **cases per day** and an **overall reduction in infection occurrences**.
>
> This could result in an annual savings to you of **$2.5 million**, based on **an improved infection rate** of **0.35%** versus last year's rate of **1.8%** (which was below the national average of 2.0%).

Figure 7.8 Customer-Focused Value Proposition Example: Healthcare

This value proposition is compelling for a CMO. Her focus is on improving the quality of patient care and improving processes so surgeons can work safely with the maximum number of patients possible. Your objective is to create a value proposition that compels the CMO to take action.

For simple sales situations, this single use of the template may be all you need. However, for sales that involve multiple people, numerous departments, and varied manifestations of business pain, you should apply this format separately for each set of stakeholders or aspect of the project, then compile them all into one powerful narrative that explains the full breadth of what your solution means to the prospect. Some sellers also like to provide tables and graphs that demonstrate when the client's investment will reach the breakeven point and the total return on investment over time. You may even want to tailor a customer-focused value proposition for presentation to the relevant executive for the sales opportunity you are pursuing. Think about how powerful that can be!

A quick and easy way to experiment with this concept is to talk to the relevant executive in the client organization which you recently sold to and ask her to help you fill in the blanks. Here's a step-by-step guide for doing this:

- Review the roles that are upstream and downstream from the department that bought your solution and are affected by it.
- Agree how long it takes the client to perform key tasks today, the quality or volume of that production, and whatever other metrics apply to the problems the client is trying to remedy.
- Establish the improvements anticipated from your solution. Try to attach a dollar figure to improved production, improved quality, and/or time saved.
- Then review the quality of the information you've gathered and compare it to the way you write value propositions today.

If you see the potential to elevate your game, adopt this approach for every new sale you get involved in. You will then be giving executives the information about value in the format they want it in, and you will sell more as a result.

3. Value Statement

The third time you talk to the client about value is after he's purchased your solution and you're now his account manager. This is when it's time to audit what you've done for your client and quantify a *value statement*. Like a quarterly frequent flyer statement, this shows all the points you've helped the client accrue as a result of his mileage with you. Remember how executives told us that they value salespeople who are willing to be accountable? This is where the rubber hits the road.

Arriving at real numbers for a value statement requires some detective work. This is why it's so important that you quantify the numbers when you describe the initial value proposition—if you don't quantify the client's pain before you install a solution, nobody will remember those numbers by the time you get around to calculating the value you delivered and describing it in a value statement.

A value statement is best delivered to the relevant executive and other key stakeholders, and is framed along the following lines:

You wanted to do Z, which we budgeted at a cost of $1 million, but it actually cost 10 percent more in out-of-scope work that nobody anticipated. We discounted that extra work by 20 percent, saving you $20,000. Within four months of starting, 100 people were using our solution and enjoying time savings and increased productivity. These users tell us that you recouped your initial cost two months faster than the eight months anticipated, adding $350,000 to your bottom line in the first year. Since we've been working with Department A, we helped solve Issue B for Executive C, and we identified two other projects for additional value that have helped your factory ship 1,000 products in the same time it used to take to ship 500 products. This has added $2.7 million directly to your top line and grown your market share by three percent. Since you announced this approach in your press meetings, analysts lifted your share price, and your improved borrowing status has saved you $750,000 in interest and allowed you to add 20 channels in Country D, which your CFO reports will add $6 million in sales this year. Our solutions represent an investment of $1,080,000, from which you have reaped gross revenues of $9.8 million, an ROI of nine dollars for every one invested with us. Now here are our ideas for building on this next year . . .

A well-written value statement is a powerful arrow, but one that our studies suggest most salespeople never remove from their quiver.

One reason they don't is that a delivery team often assumes responsibility for account management, with the salesperson remaining in a hunter role. When no obvious account manager is assigned, it's highly recommended that *someone* be appointed to read through the sales documentation that helped win the deal and look for a measurement of the problem or opportunity behind the customer's breakthrough initiative. Being able to quantify this is the starting point for calculating a statement of the value delivered.

Another reason that a value statement might not be presented is that the delivery team and/or the account manager fails to keep in contact with the key stakeholders. It's a common lament of customers that their rep comes calling only when she smells a deal brewing. Clearly, a value statement is not a tool used by transactional Commodity Suppliers.

But if you aspire to become a Trusted Advisor so that you can leverage past sales into future sales, going back over old ground and digging out the details is worth its weight in gold—or oil. There are numerous tales of entrepreneurs buying what were considered to be the worthless tailings of a gold mine that was long since spent. By carefully digging through areas known to be productive in the past, they find nuggets that evaded detection on the first pass. For example, look at the unexpected boom experienced in Alberta, Canada, when people found that they could extract oil from the dirt of old oilfields, dirt which some analysts estimate holds oil equivalent to eight times the reserves in Saudi Arabia![2]

A well-crafted value statement will help you mine a deeper well of executive credibility, possibly gaining a great customer testimonial and a renewed right to pitch your next *value hypothesis* for new business, which in turn can lead to discoveries of remarkable revenue growth.

Formal Value Reviews

While a value statement is presented in a document to a single executive, a *formal value review* will typically be aimed at multiple executives, covering a wider range of content. After you have installed a solution in a client's organization and it's been functioning for some time, make time to bring different senior executives together from across the client's business and conduct a formal value review to explore and agree on the value you have delivered. In order to do that, you will need to determine the precise metrics you'll measure in advance of the installation so you can establish benchmarks and then track and confirm the uplift. You will also want to take time in the meeting with the executives to review the steps taken to address issues and resolve problems during the implementation process.

After this initial meeting, you should seek ways to reconnect with the executives on a scheduled basis, annually at a minimum, to conduct these formal value reviews to confirm the value you are continuing to deliver to them and to their company.

You can use this meeting to expand the depth and breadth of your relationships within the client organization. For example, look for other ways to provide value to them at the beginning of their next buying cycle. Look to become viewed as a business resource to them in this regard. In addition, always look to include multiple other executives in the client organization to expand the depth and breadth of your reach so that these other executives know about you and your company.

Example of a Formal Value Review

An executive shared with us how the formal value review concept was introduced to his business from one of her major suppliers. The supplier called this program the "Customer Annual Progress Summary" (CAPS). Each year, the account manager was required to conduct a CAPS session with client executives one level above where they normally sold. The salesperson compiled a detailed formal presentation to communicate the value her company had delivered during the past year, plus the projected value for the year ahead of all projects and applications already installed. Note, this wasn't a pitch of new opportunities being considered, only what the client had already purchased or licensed.

Before the presentation was shown to the client, the supplier mandated it be reviewed by up to two levels of their own management team, to ensure it represented their official position. They also had a rule that after each CAPS, the salesperson had to return to her office to certify the review had taken place, and document detailed feedback from the meeting. This information was used to brief the customer support teams and other specialists who served as touchpoints into multiple layers and locations of the client's organization.

Several executives in the client organization were invited to attend each CAPS session. They looked forward to them as an opportunity to take a "top-down" look at their business with the assistance of someone looking in from the outside. As the client's business was discussed in terms of its emerging needs, the discussion invariably uncovered ways they could leverage their existing investment by adding new services and product capabilities, or taking what the supplier was doing in one department or country to other locations.

Of course, the executive knew a CAPS session would help his supplier identify opportunities to expand their presence across the organization. But they didn't see it as an exercise in cross-selling. They saw it as an exercise in business partnership.

Here was a reliable supplier that got along with their people, fit the culture, knew the company's quirks, satisfied all legal, administrative, and technical standards, had clocked up shared history, stood should-to-shoulder through various crises, and had a significant base of equipment installed. The client executive saw it as "good business" to build on that foundation. In fact, they believed it meant less risk and disruption to do so than to introduce new suppliers. The larger the supply contract grew, the better the supplier gained expertise in the organization's unique requirements, and the more an economy of scale was achieved.

Think about what this type of review could mean to you and your company as a way to communicate your past and current value, position you for future business, and achieve competitive immunity.

CHAPTER SUMMARY

Let's summarize what we've discussed in this chapter about the fourth question in our research: "How do you create value at the executive level?" Let's break it down to the top four messages:

1. *Plan your meetings*. Too many sales calls are planned in the parking lot five minutes before a meeting. You can't afford to bluff your way through an executive sales call. Structure the call so that it has a clear and compelling *introduction*. Be prepared to discuss the homework you've done on the executive's *issues* and their *implications* for his business and for him personally. Have an opinion about the *solution options* available from your company and show your accountability and credibility for making things happen. Plan in advance what you want to get out of the meeting and what suggestions you want to extend to the executive for *moving forward*. Executives like to be asked to take action and feel that meetings are a waste of their time if they don't produce a definitive outcome.

2. *Explore cause and effect*. Your questioning strategy needs to focus on understanding the executive's issues and the implications if her vision is not met. You need to measure the depth, severity, and immediacy of those issues and to gauge the executive's will to make a change. Ask who first identified the need for change and what happened to make exploring this need a priority over other issues. Use your knowledge of the customer's business and your own product or service to identify whether the client is focused on the root cause or just on one of the ways it manifests. Is she dealing with the real issues, or is she merely putting a finger in the dike? You will add significant value to her thought process by mapping the cause and

effect, the things that are critical to get right versus the "nice-to-haves," the stakeholders who need a voice in the solution, and how well the ideas she's already entertained will actually be equal to the need. This is an opportunity for you to reengineer the scope of projects and be seen as a thought leader.

3. *Sell your value three times.* Given that you've done your homework on the executive's company and the drivers affecting it, at the start of a sale you should have a *value hypothesis* suggesting that you have value to contribute. But you don't know for sure that you have value until you can bounce the issues around with the executive and his key stakeholders. After spending time with them, you should know enough about how the business is run now and how your solution will change things to form a *customer-focused value proposition.* To begin development of that type of value proposition, remember to include your three elements of value—your personal value, the value of your company's resources, and, lastly, the value of your company's solutions. Seek to use this process to differentiate your value from that of your competitors. Ask for the business, then be accountable for returning to measure the impact, and close the loop with the executive by presenting your *value statement.* Doing so will earn you credibility and may prime the pump for your next sales opportunity.

4. *Conduct Formal Value Reviews on a regular basis.* Look for ways to communicate the past value you have delivered to the customer organization. Don't assume that executives know the value you have created and delivered to them but realize that executives are almost always willing to meet with you

to understand your value contribution. Go back to Figure 1.1 in Chapter 1 and be reminded that executives want to get involved in the buying process by measuring the results (of the solution you have delivered). It's like a free ticket for you to the executive suite. Executives at every level—including CEOs who want to go back to their board and show them the return on their investment that they have secured by the implementation of your solution—will want to meet with you.

Chapter 8

Cultivating Loyalty at the C-Suite

Client loyalty can be achieved only if relationships are consistently built and nurtured. People at the three levels of an organization (operations, middle management, and executive) have different perspectives on you, your company, and your company's solutions.

As was pointed out in Chapter 6, "How to Establish Credibility with the C-Suite," people at the operations level focus on getting the lowest price and the steepest discounts. They also want to hear the technical details of your solution so that they can compare you with your competitors and select the lowest price. Nowhere in the conversation is there any mention of value and loyalty.

At the middle management level of the organization, people want to understand how your solution can be integrated into their organization. But while their questions will be broader in nature than those posed at the operations level, they still don't focus on value and loyalty.

It's only at the executive level of the organization that the focus is on value and that loyalty can be cultivated. Executives understand how value is created and delivered, and they fully understand the true value of loyalty. Loyal relationships are important at the executive level—and most executives are open to the cultivation of those types of relationships.

In his book *The Loyalty Effect: The Hidden Force behind Growth, Profits, and Lasting Value* (Boston: Harvard Business Review Press, 2001), Bain & Co. director Frederick F. Reichheld uses examples from State Farm and Toyota/Lexus to illustrate that loyal clients lead to substantial profitability over the long term.

According to Reichheld:

One common barrier to better loyalty and higher productivity is the fact that a lot of business executives, and virtually all accounting departments, treat income and outlays as if they occurred in separate worlds. The truth is, revenues and costs are inextricably linked, and decisions that focus on one or the other—as opposed to both—often misfire.

Companies cannot succeed or grow unless they can serve their customers with a better value proposition than the competition. Measuring customer and employee loyalty can accurately gauge the weaknesses in a company's value proposition and help to prescribe a cure.

While every loyalty leader's strategy is unique, all of them build on the following eight elements:

1. Building a superior customer value proposition
2. Finding the right customers
3. Earning customer loyalty
4. Finding the right employees
5. Earning employee loyalty
6. Gaining cost advantage through superior productivity
7. Finding the right capital sources
8. Earning their loyalty

Reichheld found that those clients who give greater loyalty typically generate more profit over the lifetime of their patronage. We agree. Increased profitability from customer retention occurs because:

- Acquisition costs are incurred only at the beginning and are amortized over the life of the relationship.
- Long-term customers provide annuities and are less sensitive to annual price increases, within reason.
- As trust is developed, referrals follow.
- Purchases of add-on products and upgrades are a natural extension over time.
- Regular customers require less education, and repeat exposure allows the seller to build expertise with each client.

But as our own research consistently found, typically there is a gap between the value you deliver and what the executives think you delivered. In Chapter 6, "How to Establish Credibility with the C-Suite," we observed that this could happen because, although the supplier has done an outstanding job, nobody bothers to tell the executive about it!

Having coached the world's largest companies, it never fails to surprise us how businesses that are so smart in most things can be so cavalier in how they look after their customer relationship management. There's a certain lemminglike behavior we see, with companies calling their salespeople "account managers" without giving much thought to what "account" and "manager" really mean. When these companies weight the sales commissions and bonuses of account managers to favor the pursuit and capture of new customers, the account managers adopt a sell-and-run mentality. By default, the customer relationship is transferred to the delivery team, whose members are usually technically proficient, but lacking in sales and service acumen.

Everybody thinks that the customer is being "account managed" because the account manager's job title suggests it. But the way the account managers are rewarded drives hunter behavior and is at odds with the mandate implied in the job title. At the end of the day, you get the behavior that you measure and reward. When customers vote with their feet, it is often to the complete astonishment of the members of the vendor's management team, who seldom recognize that their own dysfunction caused the migration and routinely slash their prices as an incentive to win the customer back.

Client executives report a strong attraction for the companies that recruit a different breed of person to farm the account (hunters and farmers are entirely different breeds, as any psychometric profile will immediately demonstrate) then remunerate the farmers for displaying appropriate behavior, and then track and communicate the value delivered. They also indicate a higher interest in remaining loyal if the recent positive experiences remain consistent over time.

If the recent experience exceeds expectations, customer loyalty is likely to be high. Loyalty can also be high even with poor performance if the expectations were originally set low; if switching costs are high; if there are no alternatives; if the social, cultural, or ethnic relationship is not easily replaced; or if there are other lock-ins such as contractual terms, shared technology, economic codependence, or a geographical imperative to retain the same suppliers even though they do only an average job.

As shown earlier in this book, senior executives typically get involved in the buying cycle for major decisions at two specific times: early in the buying process to set the overall project strategy, and also, more importantly, late in the buying cycle to measure the results and understand the value delivered by the solution provider. At this postimplementation stage, executive buyers expect the salesperson to provide regular input, report any barriers they need the executive to remove, and quantify the value delivered to the executive's business. Communicating the value delivered differentiates them from competitors and is a foundation for client loyalty.

Aim to build loyalty at (or connected to) the executive level because this is where you can obtain the best leverage. Senior executives have a companywide view of the organization and will typically ask questions that are focused on value and the return on investment of your solution, whereas lower-level executives may be focused only on price and discounts within their own department.

In his book *All for One: 10 Strategies for Building Trusted Client Partnerships* (John Wiley & Sons, 2009), Andrew Sobel talks about the competitive advantage of cultivating loyal customers:

> Loyalty, in the complex world of business-to-business relationships, is based on a subtle blend of demonstrated value added, personal trust and reciprocity.

STEPS IN CULTIVATING CLIENT LOYALTY

Cultivating client loyalty is a methodical process that combines the business and personal aspects of the relationship. Asking executives appropriate questions as you advance the business discussion may uncover areas of common interest as a foundation for a personal relationship. It's important to gauge the extent to which the executive is interested in having a social relationship beyond meetings that only focus on "talking shop."

There are some salespeople who focus only on the business relationship and keep a "professional distance" from the customer. A few industries demand a degree of aloofness be preserved to avoid any impropriety in the buyer–seller relationship. So on one side of this issue we see salespeople who cannot legally build this rapport. There are others who are under no restrictions, want to develop a personal relationship, but don't know what social chitchat appeals to an executive. And there are yet more who have no interest in building any social currency, who prefer to keep their dialogue more clinical and focused on processes, performance, and ROI.

On the flipside of this are salespeople who operate entirely in the party zone, who escalate from grabbing a coffee, to having a lunch, to hitting a bar after-hours; who are able to shift gears from walking with the executive on the floor of a business exhibition to walking the fairway of a golf course together. During this courtship they get comfortable enough to exchange amusing memes and videos, and a new friendship is born. In the most extreme examples, the salesperson will do anything to preserve this social relationship and may even start to feel it demeans the relationship to ask her new friend to actually buy anything from her.

Where you want to operate is somewhere in the middle. As you learn what's important to the executive, you may from time to time get a glimpse of how his personal motivations can be advanced by his business goals. Finding ways to address his personal and business agendas at the same time is a central theme when building

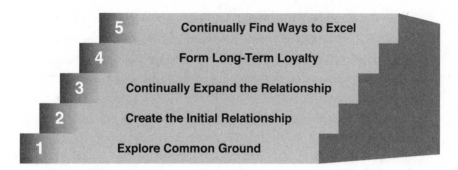

Figure 8.1 The Loyalty Staircase

loyalty. Even if you can't deliver results right away, showing that you think this way may be enough for the executive to keep you close.

So how can you do this?

It's like climbing the steps of a staircase—*a Loyalty Staircase*—where simple actions on the lower steps provide a foundation for ascending to the next step until you reach the top (see Figure 8.1). This is a tried-and-tested approach used by the world's most successful salespeople, and, importantly, it is validated by the executives themselves as what they reward salespeople for doing.

Now let's go climbing . . .

Step 1. Explore Common Ground

Client executives expect you to know what's important to them—so make certain that you do your homework not just before your initial meeting with them, but after they become a customer. Here are a few ideas:

- LinkedIn is a good place to start if you haven't met the executive yet. See where they've worked before and whether you or anyone in your sales team shares her company, industry, or geographic history. Do you share any of the same personal connections?

Have you attended the same schools or belonged to the same associations? Do you follow the same online groups or forums? Even if you don't now, you might start to follow the same things that the executive does, if only for a short time. This allows you to see some of the same posts that hit her in-box. From time to time you might see her comment, which reveals something about her attitude and affords you an opportunity to join the same conversation.

- Go to the client's website and access the last few annual reports. Within each annual report, pay special attention to a section called the "President's Letter to Shareholders" or similar title. This document contains a treasure trove of information about the key business and industry drivers, along with some of the initiatives that the company has put in place to address those drivers. Most salespeople focus on trying to dissect the annual report and drill down on the company's financials (which are important). However, the President's Letter offers a much clearer perspective on the company's important and immediate business issues. In these you may find common ground between what they are on the record as wanting to achieve and what your company can do.

- Access business, financial, and industry sites that allow you to compare how this company stacks up against its competitors in the same industry. Some of those sites are listed in Appendix A of this book, *Guide to Client Discovery*. Look for how your client compares with other companies in the same industry with respect to profitability, growth, and other important business metrics. They may be a leader that wants to maintain their dominance, a smaller player hoping for a bigger slice of pie, or a company that's falling off the mountain and grasping for a handhold. Regardless of which direction they're moving in, you can show common ground by sharing how your own company was once in the same situation and achieved the same goals, or by showing how the work you've done for other clients contributed in some way to stability, growth, or a turnaround.

- If they're a public company, listen to or read the transcripts from their quarterly earnings calls to financial analysts, as these offer insight and analysis. Typically, these calls are run by teleconference or webinar and can be found on the company website, Yahoo Finance, or similar locations. They begin with a company's investor relations officer reading a safe harbor statement to limit the company's liability should actual results prove different from the indicators they report. Then one or more company officials, often CEO and CFO, will discuss the operational results and financial statements for the period just ended and share their outlook for the upcoming period. The call is then opened for questions by investors, financial analysts, and other delegates. Granted, what the company officers say is based on rehearsals they've run to anticipate and answer the most likely analyst questions. Yet despite the semiscripted format, this is an ideal source to learn about current and emerging business issues you may not see listed anywhere else. It's another source for finding common ground about how you might help.
- A company's marketing department may produce media profiles on their executives, plus a list of recent speeches, keynotes, or webinars. These can reveal more information to help you find common ground.

Step 2. Create the Initial Relationship

You already know the importance of making a positive first impression when you start any relationship. It's even more important after you win your first sale with an executive. This is where rubber hits the road and they get to see if what you promise is the same as what you deliver. This isn't about reality but about impressions. Make certain your solution will create and deliver what you said it will and that you have a comprehensive implementation plan to exceed their expectation. Go above and beyond the service level agreement. Delight them. Do everything possible to deliver an experience that's as flawless as it can be. You never get a second chance to make a first impression—so make it count.

Executives tell us that overcommunicating in the early stage of a relationship is better than undercommunicating (or worse, making *them* chase *you*). As you shift from talking to them with your sales hat on to working as a cog in their business machine, ask how they like information delivered beyond the formal reports and score-cards. Whether they like a regular phone call, monthly meetings, or a concise e-mail, your objective is to keep the executive updated on the key issues and obstacles you face in their organization (and yours), how you plan to resolve them, and what help you need them to give from time to time. Don't deliver only the good news. Tell them what's really going on.

Step 3. Continually Expand the Relationship

"Land and expand" is where you take the corporate relationship up, down, and sideways. Executives confirm that it fills them with greater confidence if a supplier is seen working effectively with people across the enterprise. This may sound like a paradox if past experience trying to sell to clients has taught you they try to restrict how many people you contact. But that's when you're on the out-side looking in.

When you're on the inside already, it's actually in the customer's interest for you to be as active with their people as possible, where relevant to the work you're undertaking for them. In fact, the more people you talk to in the executive's company, the better they can monitor the quality of your work and the content of your conversa-tions. The grapevine is one of the informal reporting mechanisms they tap into.

So you might volunteer to work with lower-level managers or ancillary departments who are users of your product or service or benefit from it being in place. Sometimes the executive will refer you to people whose relevance you don't immediately recognize. Always accept these invitations, but ask the executive to make this introduction so it's not a cold call. Their subordinate now understands their boss sent you to meet them. It's an endorsement. Make certain you exploit both sides of that internal relationship.

Once you are committed to an expanded level of relationship in the executive's vertical silo, you should expand the relationship laterally to include other executives in other silos. You never know where the next opportunity for your solution may lie—it could be in a different functional area, in another part of the country, in another part of the world, or even in another company if the executive sits on several boards. Your reputation for delivering value is what you should be leveraging.

So always exceed expectations in all areas—large and small—and honor your commitments no matter how small they seem. Simply returning phone calls on a timely basis and going the extra mile when you respond to the executive's questions can go a long way toward increasing the executive's perception that you always conduct yourself in a businesslike manner.

Always listen to your client's issues and problems before you propose any solution. Make certain that you are seen as always adding personal value using your company's resources and offering your company's solutions that create value. If necessary, offer partner resources when you don't have a complete solution. And, lastly, make certain that you clearly and consistently communicate the value of your solutions—never assume that the executive fully understands the value that you deliver. In fact, you should always conduct an annual meeting with selected client executives specifically to communicate the value you have delivered during that year and your expectations for the coming year.

Step 4. Form Long-Term Loyalty

Beware of overconfidence when it comes to customer loyalty at the C-Suite. Gartner and ZDNet report that 89 percent of companies claimed they would compete primarily on the basis of an "enhanced customer experience" in 2016.[1] In 2017, 80 percent of these companies were beating their chests in the belief they had actually delivered a superior experience. Yet when customers were surveyed, only 8 percent felt they'd seen a loyalty-inspiring experience.[2]

This gap is the result of a growing divide between B2B suppliers still doing what worked perfectly well in the twentieth century, and the new generation of C-Suite leaders demand something else. With companies around the world losing more than US$300 billion as a result of customer churn, Frost & Sullivan predict that by 2020 "the customer experience" will overtake "price and product" as the main differentiator.[3]

How can you get on this train?

The first thing is to realize C-Suite buyers are undergoing a technology-enabled shift in how they expect you to interact with them. This began in 2015 as digital natives started taking their seats at the executive table and will be a driving factor for several decades. Generation Y workers born between 1977 and 1995 will be passing through their career peak (ages 30–50) between 2007 and 2045. Generation Z workers born between 1997 and 2015 will be passing through their career peak from 2027 to 2065.

They expect timely and personalized access to you and your company's services anywhere, anytime, through any device. They expect queries to be dealt with quickly by an informed expert. Over 71 percent of these buyers equate how much you care with how easy you are to find and how quickly you respond to them. They want all interactions to be contextualized and personalized and for you to make it simple for them to talk or buy with less effort—60 percent even say they're happy to pay a higher fee if it delivers this.

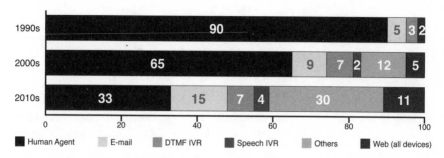

Figure 8.2 Shifting Contact Preferences in the Customer Experience

You can see in Figure 8.2 how contact preferences have changed over time.

By way of explanation, you know what is meant by "human agent" and "e-mail." "DTMF IVR" is where clients dial a number, and the key tones from their dial pad lead them through a menu that conducts them to a relevant person. "Speech IVR" is a more humanized form of the same task where the client speaks instead of pressing buttons. "Web (all devices)" covers the experience executives have on your main website and your mobile-optimized single-page sites and interacting with web-based e-mail campaign landing pages, pop-up text chats, and surveys.

It's the fast-growth "Others" category you need to pay attention to. It shows a pattern of exponential growth and includes the rise of social media channels like Facebook, LinkedIn, and Twitter, and online video conferencing like WebEx, GoToMeeting, and Skype, plus other customer experience technologies driven by machine learning and artificial intelligence (AI) in pursuit of an "omni-channel experience," where a customer's interaction history allows them to start a discussion with you in one medium (like a chat window) and seamlessly complete it in another (with a phone call, for example).

The common theme here is one of personalization. Customers are no longer satisfied being grouped into a market segment with millions of users. The new segment is an audience of one.

As a sales professional, it's your job to be there for C-Suite clients where, when, and how they want to talk, without them needing to repeat things to help you catch up. If your company doesn't offer this capability, your sales may plateau through no fault of your own. But there's nothing stopping you from dipping into your own commission funds to subscribe to technology or services that allow you to offer the personalized experience that earns the fealty of the C-Suite.

This is a mindset that differentiates true sales professionals (who take responsibility for every aspect of their success) from people who "just work in a sales job." It's worth taking inventory of this from time to time. For example, what is the last book about selling you spent your own money to buy (before you wisely bought this book, of course)? When is the last time you paid to attend a training seminar on a new aspect of selling? What's the latest app you purchased to help you sell, manage your time, aggregate your social media, or engage with customers, that's not part of your company's core sales technology? Do you pay someone else to do research, create prospecting lists, send e-mails, or call customers on your behalf? Do you see yourself as an employee or as an agent of change? Are you in control of every link in the sales process that your income depends on, or do you let people and processes outside your control place your financial future at risk? If any of these questions makes you uncomfortable, that's the future calling. Respond accordingly.

Of course, beyond personalization, easier and more seamless methods of contact, and feeling respected as "an audience of one," a perennial currency that buys C-Suite loyalty is delivering on the promises you made on behalf of your company, putting out fires, measuring the value of what you've delivered, getting credit for it from the people who most influence your contract renewals and expansion to other opportunities, and bringing them new ideas to create additional value. We've covered these techniques amply in this book's other chapters.

When discussing value, always use the executive's own industry or company jargon. Quantify the time saved, problems solved, risk reduced, revenue increased, costs removed, and lives improved. Wherever you have examples of specific people's jobs getting easier and how this frees up their time or improves their effectiveness, place a value on it. Show the return on investment being achieved as a result of your company delivering the promises you made in past sales. Consider asking your company's financial experts to help you prepare and even present financial information if you're not comfortable talking about spreadsheets and using accounting language.

Step 5. Continually Find Ways to Excel

As you continue to enhance the client relationship, you have multiple opportunities to add value. Doing so consistently allows you to advance from Commodity Supplier to Emerging Resource, then to a Problem Solver subject matter expert all the way up to Trusted Advisor where you come to be seen as a consultant to the executive at a personal level as much as a business level. A way to measure this is by contemplating the questions they ask you in each interaction. Are they focused only on the project or service you're delivering, or do they range to other areas? When an executive starts asking your opinion about issues unrelated to your company's core work, it's never a bad sign.

So how should you work with client executives when things go wrong, there are unforeseen delays, your product doesn't work as promised, and relationships get strained between the client, you, and your company? Do you vanish behind the scenes to solve the problem, with the intent of calling after you've put out the fire? No. Make yourself highly visible as soon as possible to the client executive, showing him that you understand his pain and you're working on his behalf to get things on track. Make certain that you're visible as an active player when things aren't going well. It's even better if you see the problem before it happens, and give the client executive advance warning along with an explanation of how the situation will be resolved. Nobody likes surprises.

A head office executive told us of a salesperson who had sold his company a multimillion dollar mainframe which was installed at their largest manufacturing plant. That computer had quickly become an integral part of the company's business: scheduling the plant floor, ordering the right supplies, and controlling the inventory. Suddenly it fell out of service and red ink started to flow. The client executive was impressed that the salesperson immediately scheduled an appointment with him and brought their branch manager, service specialists, and even flew engineers in from the client's manufacturing plant. The problem was found and the mainframe was repaired within a week. During that time, the salesperson made certain she was visible as an active participant who kept all relevant executives informed of progress. The top executive never forgot this salesperson and later told her: "You show up when things go wrong, not only when they go right." He found this willingness and proactivity in being held accountable a rare trait, which solidified the salesperson's position as a Trusted Advisor in the years that followed.

Clearly, cultivating client loyalty is achieved by consciously implementing a methodical step-by-step process as you climb the Loyalty Staircase. This begins with exploring common ground with the executive and culminates in a long-term relationship. Though carrying out this process will take time, always remember which step you are currently on so that you can optimize your position. Beyond that, you should constantly seek ways to excel—to continually differentiate the value you deliver to the client organization—so the corporate relationship can be sustained and expanded even if individual players come and go.

Executives transfer to different departments; move to new firms; and take freelance, board, or advisory roles all the time. So never be satisfied having a Trusted Advisor relationship with a single executive or in only one department. Cultivate loyalty across the client organization, expand your network, and optimize those relationships—whether in the same company or other firms executives migrate to. Even when an executive's new role is in a different industry, they may continue asking for your guidance. Executives are loyal to salespeople who bring loyalty and value to them.

CHAPTER SUMMARY

Let's summarize the top three messages in this chapter:

1. *Value drives loyalty.* Don't let your experiences with transaction-focused subordinates lead you into thinking that executives share their buying culture. While the buying culture of some companies emanates from the top, most executives told us that they are open to the idea of loyalty in the buyer–seller relationship. The currency you exchange for their loyalty is the consistent delivery of value. Like beauty, value is in the eye of the beholder, so you need to know what each executive considers valuable, consistently deliver that level of value, and make sure you get credit for your good work. If your contribution is not recognized, it holds no value for you.

2. *Climb the Loyalty Staircase.* Almost anybody can sell to an executive once, at the bottom step of a staircase. Enjoying repeated success in the C-Suite requires doing things well on a consistent basis, one step at a time. Remember to treat executives with respect, but treat them like everyday people, too. Don't fear them, and don't pander to them. Explore common ground and demonstrate what you know. You can never be guilty of overcommunication when your intent is to make a genuine contribution. It's critical that you and the members of your team focus on excellence. Nothing should be too much trouble. Demonstrate that your attitude is to serve and to make a difference. When problems occur, be the first to identify and rectify them. Show yourself as being proactive and "on the ball." As you do these things, you will be invited into the executive's circle, you will meet more of the people he confides in, and you will develop loyalty.

3. *Quantify the value.* Use the executive's industry and company metrics to explain the value you deliver. Wherever possible, quantify the value in terms of time saved, problems eliminated, risk reduced, revenue increased, or costs removed. Give examples of specific people's jobs getting easier and place a value on time, effectiveness, and efficiency improvements. Show the return on investment being achieved as a result of your company delivering the promises you made in past sales. Have your company's financial experts present complex financial information and accounting language.

Afterword

SELLING TO THE C-SUITE

In today's competitive environment, as professional salespeople strive to differentiate themselves and retain established clients, they need to constantly seek to reach higher levels in the client's organization and build long-term relationships. Selling at the executive level requires a different set of skills and strategies from selling at the more traditional departmental level or making transactional sales.

In this book, we have tried to outline strategies for creating, maintaining, and leveraging relationships with senior-level executives in your client organizations. While that sounds simple, many salespeople continue to be reluctant to call on senior-level client executives.

Let's review some of the challenges professional salespeople have in calling on senior client executives. Typically, when we pose this question to a group of professional salespeople, we tell them that we know that none of *them* have challenges in calling on client executives—so we ask them to tell us about the challenges they think some of their friends might have in calling on executives!

Interviews with thousands of top salespeople confirm the following types of challenges:

- Recognizing the importance of the *relevant* executive in the current sales campaign
- Selecting the right executive to call on
- Identifying the right approach to use in accessing the executive
- Determining the best time in the client's buying cycle to meet with the executive
- Getting past the gatekeeper
- Having an in-depth understanding of the executive's key business issues
- Being intimidated by the questions that might arise during the meeting
- Jeopardizing lower-level relationships

We can summarize those challenges as three simple issues, all of which can be addressed by the actions described in this book. Those three issues are:

- Inability to identify the relevant executive
- Lack of self-confidence and fear of failure in calling on executives
- Being blocked from getting to the relevant executive

Simply put, the actions you can take to mitigate those challenges can be summarized as thorough preparation, constant practice, and determination, combined with a degree of perseverance. Thorough preparation means that you have done your homework prior to your first encounter with a client executive, and that you have a fairly good understanding of the executive's key business issues and how your company's solutions might create value, both for that executive and for the executive's company. Through practice and determination in calling on executives at that level, you will increase your self-confidence and overcome your fear of failure. The preparation you did in advance of your meeting with the executive will also decrease the possibility of your being intimidated by the questions that an executive might pose.

Remember that each and every salesperson has had to make that initial call on a key client executive for the very first time—and that's true no matter how many sales calls a professional salesperson has made in his lifetime. And lastly, through perseverance, you will be able to navigate the political structures of the client organization to the point where you'll be a master, not only of circumventing gatekeepers, but also of pleasing key players in the organization by calling on and interfacing with the right people.

SIX CRITICAL STEPS IN CREATING, MAINTAINING, AND LEVERAGING RELATIONSHIPS WITH CLIENT EXECUTIVES

1. *Identify the relevant executive.* This entire process starts with identifying the relevant executive for the sales opportunity. Remember that we defined the relevant executive as the executive who stands to gain the most or lose the most as a result of the application or project associated with the sales opportunity. It's critical that you identify the relevant executive early in the sales cycle, so that you can maintain your focus on that key executive.
2. *Determine the best approach to get to the relevant executive.* Once a salesperson has identified the relevant executive, obtaining a meeting with that executive is typically not very difficult. Feedback from executives we surveyed indicates that they are most likely to grant a meeting to a salesperson if the request for that meeting comes from a credible source within their own organization. In fact, in the first two studies conducted, 84 percent of the executives interviewed said that they would usually or always grant a meeting if the salesperson was recommended internally.

However, the most important factor in that process is that the recommendation must come from someone whom the executive deems to be credible. If the executive does not deem the salesperson's sponsor within the client organization to be credible, the salesperson's chance of getting a meeting with the executive is considerably reduced. According to our studies, other methods of access were clearly less effective. Referrals from people outside the organization would yield a meeting approximately 50 percent of the time; however, cold calls to the executive (even those following a letter or an e-mail) worked only about 20 percent of the time.

3. *Perform the appropriate research before that critical first meeting with an executive.* Not having an in-depth understanding of the executive's key business issues could represent the single biggest stumbling block for a salesperson who's about to meet with a client executive for the first time. Executives have little or no tolerance for salespeople who have not done their homework prior to a key meeting with them. In the surveys we conducted, C-level leaders stated in very clear language that they expect the people who meet with them to have an in-depth understanding of the key business issues facing them and to listen intently before proposing any product or service solutions.

   Developing in-depth knowledge about the client is the fastest way to be able to contribute insight and create long-term collaborative relationships with senior-level client executives. As we demonstrated, client learning occurs on three levels—the client's industry, the client's company, and then, lastly, the client executive herself—and at each level you become more valuable to the client executive. Remember, Appendix A to this book contains a *Guide to Client Discovery.*

4. *Conduct an effective first meeting with the client executive.* Throughout this book, we've stressed the importance of that critical initial face-to-face meeting with a client executive. In fact, we even gave

you a template for conducting that meeting (see Figure 7.1). In any case, you need to remember that you never have a second chance to make a good first impression!

Your objective for that critical first meeting is to begin to create a lasting relationship with the client executive. To that end, your focus should not be on a short-term product sale, but on a longer-term relationship that transcends any short-term sales.

5. *Demonstrate integrity and capability in subsequent meetings, so that the executive perceives you as a Trusted Advisor.* When client executives perceive that you have demonstrated that you are reliable and trustworthy on a consistent basis, you will have achieved a level of personal integrity with them. In addition, when client executives perceive that you have demonstrated both insight and expertise, they will begin to recognize that you have a level of capability that, combined with your level of integrity, can lead to a collaborative relationship. When this happens, you will be operating in the Client Value Zone and ultimately come to be perceived as a Trusted Advisor by the client executive.

It is important to point out, however, that this level of business relationship may not be achievable with all clients. Some clients may not want this level of relationship, and you also have to understand the extent of your involvement—in terms of both time and resources—in developing a Trusted Advisor type of relationship. It may be that with some clients, this level of relationship is simply not worth the required investment. As the manager of your sales territory, you have to make that decision.

6. *Consistently communicate your value to the executive.* Don't overlook opportunities to communicate the value of your solution to the client executive. The CXO-level executives we meet continually say that they like to get involved at the end of the buying cycle to understand the value that a salesperson's solution has delivered to them.

In Figure 7.2 we clearly outlined the fact that your value has three components: the value you bring to the client's company with your background and experience, the value your company's resources bring to the client, and the value your solution brings to the client organization. Make certain that you take advantage of the opportunity to communicate those three components of value, particularly following the installation of your solution. As a salesperson, you may want to implement a formal process that ensures some level of consistent communication with client executives to review the specific value that your company delivers to them.

For example, some vendors explain to their customers that to ensure that promises are fulfilled and expectations are managed, an annual client account review meeting should be scheduled on the anniversary of signing the first contract. These meetings focus on reporting to *all* relevant executives the specific changes that have occurred in the customer's business as a result of your solution being installed. Account managers take special care to review with each stakeholder the reasons for needing a solution that he gave during the sales cycle, and his expectations for what the right solution would do for him personally, for others working in the same department, and across the business overall. With this information tucked away, you can then revisit the customer three, six, or twelve months after the deal was closed and the solution installed to measure the extent to which those original expectations are being delivered.

If expectations *are not* being met, this meeting provides an opportunity to explore the reasons why and resolve the problems; this demonstrates accountability and the ability to marshal resources (two traits that executives say they look for in their suppliers).

If expectations *are* being met *or exceeded*, the client account review is an opportunity to get credit for your good work from each stakeholder who influenced the decision. This helps prime the pump for the next opportunity, and is a key to loyalty, as discussed previously.

A FINAL WORD

Calling on senior-level client executives can be compared to learning to play golf. It takes time, effort, and a high level of energy to become proficient. Calling at the executive level is a learned skill; it's not something you're born with, and, like golf, it usually improves only with a lot of constant practice. The more times you make a certain type of shot in golf or make a key call at the executive level, the more proficient and, perhaps even more important, the more comfortable you become. You'll spend many hours practicing your skill of calling at the executive level, and after some of those experiences, you may get frustrated and feel that the efforts you have expended have not been worth it. Even the most seasoned professionals on the PGA Tour blow a shot now and then. But take it from the authors of this book, who have more than 80 years of combined sales experience in calling on executives: *There's nothing like the thrill of closing a big deal—especially when it comes with the help of that Trusted C-Suite Advisor in the client organization who was working behind the scenes to help close the deal!*

Do these things well, and you are on your way to mastering selling to the C-Suite.

Good luck with the journey!

Appendix A

Guide to Client Discovery

LEARNING ABOUT YOUR CLIENTS

There are three levels of research involved in learning about your client: research on the industry, the company, and the client executives themselves (see Figure A1.1). Knowing about your client at these three levels will help you formulate your thinking about a key call on a client executive, as well as developing an incisive, meaningful, and compelling value proposition.

The overall objective in researching a prospect or client, however, is to appear confident and credible, as well as concise as you approach the executive, especially if it is in the initial face-to-face call. All of this suggests that your research approach should be both systematic and thorough.

Here are a couple of high-level tips:

- Continually conduct background reading on industries where you spend the most time so that you can develop a working knowledge of the trends, terminology, and metrics used within the industry.
- Employ Google Alerts (google.com/alerts) and Talkwalker Alerts (talkwalker.com/alerts) to update you on industry trends and regulation changes so that you are continually aware of the latest developments.
- Utilize social media techniques such as LinkedIn, Twitter, and Facebook to monitor information on target companies and industries.
- Use your current client base for information on new developments within key industries and how they are affected by recent changes in laws and regulations.
- Gather information from company websites, accessing annual reports and reading the CEO or President's letter where you will find information such as the company mission statement, as well as the key business drivers facing the company and the business initiatives the company is implementing to address those

Figure A1.1 Three Levels of Client Research

drivers. (Perhaps you have solutions that can assist with some of those "breakthrough initiatives.")
- Consider attending an industry conference to get more in-depth knowledge about a particular industry.

To get your research rolling, here are some additional key pointers and Internet resources that should quickly guide you to the information you need.

Information on Your Client's Industry

Most executives expect sales professionals to have a certain degree of industry knowledge and expertise about their industry. In some cases, this type of knowledge will almost be second nature to the salesperson, particularly if the salesperson is only calling on clients within one specific industry (healthcare, for example). However, if you are calling on numerous industries, you have to be conversant with the issues, pressures, and trends in that client's specific industry so that you can create the most value for them.

Become vigilant about the major changes that are taking place within the industry, especially with regard to any regulatory issues that may affect your client. If you can become recognized as an industry expert by your client, it will go a long way toward being perceived as a Trusted Advisor.

Good starting points for industry trends are trade association journals or industry analyst reports to which your company may already have access. These typically include Hoovers, InsideView, First Research Inc., and other similar organizations. While all of these sites have subscription fees, they can often provide extremely valuable information and reduce the time it takes to conduct your research. Your company may already have access to some of these paid subscription sites, so it's usually best to check with your management.

Trade journals and magazines (and their associated websites) are often available at no charge and they can also provide significant and relevant information. As mentioned previously, industry association shows and conferences may be another good source of information about specific industries and your investment in participating in one or more of these types of conferences may pay great dividends.

Information on Your Client's Company

As you become more knowledgeable about your client's strategy, as well as their key business drivers and initiatives, your ability to suggest new ideas and solutions will increase dramatically.

Your understanding of the client's organizational structure will also pay huge dividends for you, particularly as you become adept at identifying the relevant executives for short- and long-range projects. At this level of learning, you'll be able to provide business value to the client's organization.

Read about your client online to develop an in-depth understanding of their business, the type of work they do, and how they stack up against other similar companies and organizations in the same industry. Determine how they are perceived by business and financial analysts and try to develop an understanding of their business plan, as well as their key business drivers. Try to ascertain how your client is positioned within their industry—are they perceived as an industry leader in any particular area, for example.

When researching your client's company, you should also focus on obtaining information about your client's customers. Who are your client's top 10 customers? What percent of your client's annual revenues come from those top 10 customers? What actions does your client take to ensure they retain those key customers? Do you have solutions that could help your client retain those key customers?

You should also develop information about your client's key competitors. Who are your client's top three competitors? What competitive advantage do each of those competitors have? What competitive advantage does your client have? What percent of market share does your client have?

What is your client doing to secure future competitive advantage? Don't shy away from asking your clients about their perspective on their top competitors so that you can get a better idea of how they perceive their standing against them. Then you can ask yourself if you have solutions that can enable your client to achieve a level of competitive advantage against those competitors.

Knowledge About the Client Executive

At the pinnacle of this pyramid is the client executive. You'll get to know and understand them both personally and professionally as the relationship grows. As you see executives navigate the political structures of their organization, you'll get a better understanding of their psyche and how to successfully sell your ideas and get them across effectively. At this level of client learning, you are in a unique position to provide extraordinary value to the executive and her company.

There are numerous ways to obtain information about individual executives, such as using a search engine to enter the executive's name accompanied by words such as *strategy, announce*, or *press release* and the current year. Adding *.pdf* and *.ppt* to your search may unearth presentations to investors or other webinars that your prospect or client company posted online and forgot to take down; these can often be downloaded and reveal the goals and issues that the executive has gone on record as supporting. Such information is golden!

You should also make use of social media and other Internet resources. LinkedIn, for example, is an extremely powerful tool for researching the executive. Prior to every call on a new executive, make it a standard practice to conduct a LinkedIn search. Simply enter the executive's name in the "Search" box on your LinkedIn home page. Check who he is connected to, where he has worked in the past, as well as the schools, universities, professional associations, and other connections he has in common with other people in his company (and yours or your competitors). What you find may reveal tribal affiliations that could be used to open doors and shape decision outcomes. Contact those people to gain information, insights, or introductions.

In addition, the executive you will be meeting with will often check you out on LinkedIn. So make certain that your LinkedIn presence is compelling, up to date, and relevant. Start with a professional photo, remembering this may be the first impression you make. Write your LinkedIn profile in the first person and make certain it accurately reflects your background, experience, and why executives should prioritize meeting you over your competitors.

INTERNET BROWSERS AND SEARCH ENGINES

The Internet provides the ability to research client organizations at three levels of learning quickly and efficiently. A *search engine* is a program accessed via a URL (e.g., www.google.com) that allows you to search for information by typing key words, phrases, or questions into a search bar. Most sites offer "Advanced Search" or similarly named options that increase the effectiveness of your search. Power users can learn how to incorporate special "operators" into their searches to target the desired information more accurately.

See www.google.com/help/refinesearch.html for an excellent guide to using operators and other advanced techniques.

There are many search engines to choose from. Here are a few of the most popular:

Google	www.google.com
Hotbot	www.hotbot.com
Lycos	www.lycos.com
MetaCrawler	www.metacrawler.com
Search	www.search.com
Webcrawler	www.webcrawler.com
Yahoo!	www.yahoo.com

BUSINESS PERIODICALS AND NEWS SERVICES

The following sites offer substantial amounts of information on company news. Browse them and bookmark the ones that are most relevant to you:

Associated Press	www.ap.org
BusinessWeek	www.businessweek.com
Computerworld	www.computerworld.com
Fast Company	www.fastcompany.com
Forbes	www.forbes.com
Fortune	www.fortune.com
Gartner Inc.	www.gartner.com

Harvard Business Review	www.hbr.org
McKinsey Quarterly	www.mckinsey.com
Newspapers of the World	www.newslink.org
PR Newswire	www.prnewswire.com
Reuters News Agency	www.reuters.com
Sales and Marketing Management	www.salesandmarketing.com
Selling Power	www.sellingpower.com
The Economist	www.economist.com
The Red Herring	www.redherring.com
Wall Street Journal	www.wsj.com

There are many sources of information available about industries and companies. Some might be considered traditional print sources, while others are on the Internet. Use a variety to research your client or prospect to see what sources are most effective in your particular sales environment. Over time, you'll develop your own approach for researching new clients and prospects, and doing it quickly.

Following is listing of additional sources of information to consider:

GUIDE TO CLIENT DISCOVERY
SOURCES OF INFORMATION

SOURCE	INFORMATION
Company Organization Charts	• Rank and Function of Key Executives • Recent Promotions and Newest Key Players
Company's Marketing Department	• Profiles of Key Executives • Features and Functions of Company's Products and Services • Recent Speeches by Key Executives
Company Websites	• Soft Copies of Annual Reports • Company Directories • Latest Company News • Company Financials • Case Studies of Key Customers • Features/Functions of Company's Products/ Services
Quarterly Earnings Call and Annual Investor Briefings (Often Available as Videos)	• Results from Previous Quarter • Outlook of Future Results • Insightful Questions from Financial Analysts • Note: Access company website for details
Annual Reports	• Chairman's Letter • Key Financials • Company Directions and Trends • Company's Position in the Industry • New Products and Services • Executive Team/Board of Directors
10K (Last year) **10Q** (Last quarter) Note: These are U.S. filing forms. Find your country's equivalent (e.g., the AIF in Canada or Companies House AR01 in the UK).	• Profiles of Key Executives • Key Financials • Top Competitors • Details Beyond the Annual Report
Reports from Financial Analysts	• Investment Perspectives and Outlook • Industry Comparisons • Product and Service Analysis

GUIDE TO CLIENT DISCOVERY
SOURCES OF INFORMATION, *continued*

SOURCE	INFORMATION
Company/Departmental Newsletters/Press Releases	• Latest Company Events • Recent Promotions • Philanthropic Ventures • New Key Assignments and New Hires • Features and Functions of Company's Latest Products and Services
Company Investor Relations Department	• Key Financials • Executive Team • Latest Company Events • Product and Service Offerings
Newspapers/Magazines	• Recent Articles • Excerpts from Key Speeches • Latest Industry Trends
News About Your Clients	• Instant Updates on Articles Recently Published About Your Specific Client and the Client's Industry • Excerpts from Recent Speeches by Client Executives • News About Client Executives • Google Alerts/Talkwalker Alerts
Online Services and Other Internet Sites	• Free or Fee-Based • Profiles of Key Executives • Company Financials • Company Position Within Industry • Industry Trends • Company Outlook • Vast Array of Information
Industry and Association Meetings	• Company's Top Competitors • Company's Position Within the Industry • Company's Presence Versus Their Competitors • Industry Trends
Blogs	• Public Information • Customer Experiences • Recent News • Public Opinions

PUTTING IT ALL TOGETHER

Now that you have an idea of some of the traditional sources of information, we'll put them in perspective regarding the three levels of learning. Here are some of the sources to consider regarding each level of client learning.

LEARNING	SOURCE
Consolidating Information About Your Client's Industry	• Online Services and Other Internet Sites • Industry and Association Meetings/Conferences • Google Alerts/Talkwalker Alerts • InsideView, Hoovers, First Research • Newspapers/Magazines • Reports from Financial Analysts
Consolidating Information About Your Client's Company	• Company Organization Charts • Company's Marketing Department • Company Websites • Quarterly Earnings Call • Annual Reports/10K/10Q • Reports from Financial Analysts • Company/Departmental Newsletters/Press Releases • InsideView, Hoovers, First Research • Company Investor Relations Department • Newspapers/Magazines • Google Alerts/Talkwalker Alerts • Online Services and Other Internet Sites
Consolidating Information About the Client Executive	• Company Organization Charts • Company's Marketing Department • Company Websites • Annual Reports/10K/10Q • Company/Departmental Newsletters/Press Releases • Newspapers/Magazines • Google Alerts/Talkwalker Alerts • Online Services and Other Internet Sites • LinkedIn/Twitter/Facebook

PREPARING FOR THE INITIAL FACE-TO-FACE
CALL ON A CLIENT EXECUTIVE

Now that you understand that you have to conduct research on your client's industry, your client's company, and the client executive, you'll want to start consolidating that information so that you can conduct an intelligent first conversation with a client executive.

The worksheet shown below helps you capture the type of information that you'd typically want to have at your fingertips prior to that first critical conversation with the client. This will enable you to be perceived by the client executive as a thought leader who's both professional and prepared. In addition, you can use this information to develop key questions to pose to the client executive.

Remember, it's better to first show the executive that you've done homework on her company and industry, then use that information to probe her for insights you can't retrieve from a public source. This shows the executive you respect her time enough to arrive prepared for a conversation that avoids "dumb-dumb" questions and instead challenges her thinking as would a business peer.

Examples of Information You Should Know
Before a First Meeting

What are the most recent trends in the executive's industry?

What is his company's position in the industry (leader, follower, growing, declining)? How does his company metrics compare with the industry leaders?

What is the executive's goal or mission?

What are his company's key business drivers and initiatives? What is the executive's breakthrough initiative, and what is compelling him to change from the status quo?

What payback will the company achieve if this initiative is implemented, or what consequences will they suffer as a result of not implementing this initiative?

What questions will you ask the executive on your initial call?

What points do you want to make (to get credit for doing your homework)?

_____

_____

_____

_____

What solution(s) can you offer that will affect the breakthrough initiative?

_____

_____

_____

_____

Tools for Building the Executive Relationship

SALES OPPORTUNITY PROFILE

SALESPERSON	CLIENT

SALES OPPORTUNITY	EXPECTED REVENUE

Describe the client's application or project.

What is the basis for your pursuit of this opportunity?

Outline the solution that will enable you to effectively compete for this opportunity.

Can you win this opportunity by calling on executives with whom you've already established a relationship? If NO, who else will you need to establish a relationship with?

Who is the relevant executive for this sales opportunity?

How will you gain access to that executive?

INITIAL EXECUTIVE TELEPHONE CALL PLANNER

INTRODUCTION	
• Provide a brief introduction of you and your company. • Explain your connection to the person who referred you to the executive, if appropriate.	
PURPOSE	
Be clear, concise, and specific as you explain the reason you are contacting the executive.	
CREDIBILITY	
Explain the homework you've done on the organization and communicate how you've helped other companies address similar challenges.	
COMMITMENT TO ACTION	
Propose a clear and specific action for the executive to take.	

ROADBLOCK WORKSHEET

Which executive are you attempting to access?
Why does the roadblock exist?
What are the risks associated with attempting to gain access to the relevant executive?
What are the risks (short-term and long-term) of not getting to the relevant executive in this sales campaign?
What will you do?

BUSINESS ISSUES WORKSHEET

DRIVERS	
What are the internal or external factors that might cause the client to change or react?	
TWO INTERNAL FACTORS	
Financial	Operational
SIX EXTERNAL FACTORS	
Customers	Competitors
Suppliers	Business Partners
Regulatory Issues	Globalization

PROPOSE A CLEAR AND SPECIFIC ACTION FOR THE EXECUTIVE TO TAKE
What is the most important initiative the client must act upon? It is typically bound by a time frame and accompanied by significant payback or consequences.

ISSUES IMPACTING THE BREAKTHROUGH INITIATIVE

YOUR SOLUTION
• How does your solution address the breakthrough initiative and provide payback? • How can you differentiate the value of your solution?

EXECUTIVE-LEVEL MEETING PLANNER

INTRODUCTION	
• Refer to your initial telephone call with the executive. • Cite your past experience.	

ISSUES AND IMPLICATIONS	
• Ask questions that confirm your level of preparation. • Discuss the issues and implications. • Confirm the importance of the breakthrough initiative.	

SOLUTION OPTIONS	
• Explore potential solutions. • Develop a vision of the optimal solution. • Confirm the value of the solution.	

MOVING FORWARD	
• Reconnect with the executive to secure return access. • Create an action plan that involves the executive.	

VALUE PROPOSITION WORKSHEET

You should be capable of _____ by _____
                        describe the impact   monetary units
                                                      or %

through the ability to _____ .
                        describe the new situation

This will require an investment of _____ ,
                                    state the cost of the solution

which will be returned within _____ .
                               estimate the time frame for return

We recently implemented a similar solution at

_____ , who achieved _____ .
     name of client   specific savings achieved

EXECUTIVE PRESENTATION GUIDE—PAGE 1

COMPANY NAME/ PRESENTATION DATE	ACCOUNT MANAGER NAME/PHONE
NAME OF RELEVANT EXECUTIVE	TITLE AND RESPONSIBILITIES
APPLICATION/PROJECT	IMPACT OF THIS PROJECT ON THE RELEVANT EXECUTIVE

Describe Our Solution for This Project	
Background of the Relevant Executive (Previous Jobs/Company Affiliations)	Recent Key Decisions Made
Universities Attended and Degrees Received	Affiliations with Other Company Boards
Relevant Executive's Decision Criteria for This Project	
Executive's Business Agenda or Focus	Executive's Personal Agenda or Focus

OTHER CLIENT EXECUTIVES EXPECTED TO PARTICIPATE IN THE PRESENTATION		
Name	Title	Responsibilities

ADDITIONAL PARTICIPANTS FROM OUR COMPANY	
Name	Phone

EXECUTIVE PRESENTATION GUIDE—PAGE 2

KEY ISSUES THAT MIGHT ARISE DURING THE PRESENTATION

MAJOR COMPETITORS AND THE SOLUTION(S) THEY MAY OFFER

OUR RELATIONSHIP WITH THE RELEVANT EXECUTIVE
What do we think is our current level of relationship with the relevant executive? ☐ Commodity Supplier ☐ Emerging Resource ☐ Problem Solver ☐ Trusted Advisor
What actions have we taken (with this client and specifically with this executive) to achieve that level of relationship?
What specific actions has the relevant executive implemented or taken to demonstrate this level of relationship?

EXECUTIVE PRESENTATION GUIDE—PAGE 3

Presenting Your Solution to the Executive

INTRODUCTION/PRESENTATION OBJECTIVES

Outline the objectives of the presentation and confirm the overall agenda.

ISSUES AND IMPLICATIONS

Describe the project or application, making certain you demonstrate a clear understanding of the key issues facing the executive.

SOLUTION OPTIONS

Explore potential solutions and their value to both the executive and the company.

EXECUTIVE PRESENTATION GUIDE—PAGE 4

Presenting Your Solution to the Executive

CONTRAST THE VALUE OF YOUR PROPOSED SOLUTION

Develop a graphical picture of the current approach and contrast it with your proposed solution to dramatically depict the differences, as well as the additional value.

MOVING FORWARD—SUGGESTED NEXT STEPS

Outline the next steps, as well as your expectations for the executive's involvement in those next steps. (This is your way of securing return access.)

EXECUTIVE PRESENTATION GUIDE—PAGE 5

Post-Call

☐ Was your presentation focused on the relevant executive and the executive's company?
- Did it clearly demonstrate an understanding of the executive's key business issues?
- Did you contrast the current approach and the approach of your proposed solution?
- Were the differences clear, and was the proposed solution dramatically better?
- Did you clearly articulate your specific business value, and did it include you and your company as well as your solution?
- Did you present a plan for moving forward, and did that plan clearly involve the executive in multiple steps or stages?

☐ Did you involve the appropriate key personnel from the client organization in developing the presentation to the relevant executive?

☐ Were you able to collect appropriate information about the relevant executive and thoroughly analyze it before preparing your presentation?

☐ Did you communicate that information to your team before the presentation to the executive?

☐ Prior to the presentation, did you try to assign each member of your team to a corresponding member of the client team?

☐ Did you rehearse your presentation and have someone give you constructive feedback and suggestions for improvement?

☐ Did you ask for feedback about the presentation from the relevant executive before you left the meeting?

☐ Did you recognize and thank the people from the client organization who helped you develop the presentation?

☐ Did you ask and get feedback from those same people about their reaction to the presentation?

☐ Do you have a plan to reconnect with the relevant executive in a timely fashion to keep the momentum of the project moving forward?

RELEVANT EXECUTIVE CALL PLAN

CLIENT	DATE OF INITIAL MEETING

NAME OF *RELEVANT EXECUTIVE*	POSITION

SALESPERSON NAME	INITIAL SALES OPPORTUNITY

Have we identified the relevant executive for the sales opportunity within this client organization? The relevant executive is defined as the executive who stands to gain the most or lose the most as a result of the application or project associated with our sales opportunity. Typically there is one relevant executive in the client organization for a specific sales opportunity; however, if you have multiple opportunities within the same organization, each opportunity may have a unique relevant executive.

PRIOR TO THE CALL	
About the *Relevant Executive* and Client Organization • Who have we identified as the *relevant executive* and what is his or her formal role and responsibility in the organization? • How is he or she measured and rewarded? • What decisions can this executive influence or make independently? • Who is in his or her influence network? • Whose influence network is he or she in? • Does he or she have affiliations with other companies? • Where was the executive they hired from (previous companies—if applicable)? • Who does the *relevant executive* report to and what is the relationship between those two individuals?	

RELEVANT EXECUTIVE CALL PLAN, *continued*

Business Pressures and Initiatives • What are the internal and external pressures driving the need for change (e.g., Financial, Operational, Competitive, Customer, Supplier, Business Partner, and the like)? • Which key business objective is most important to the relevant executive and why? • What are the plans or initiatives the client has put in place to address these significant business pressures? • Is the application or project associated with our sales opportunity linked with a key business initiative? • How could we make an impact on our client's business and/or help them address this key business initiative?	
Known or Anticipated Obstacles • What obstacles are known or anticipated? From whom? Why? How can they be addressed and mitigated in advance? • Is there any history with this client that might impact their perceptions of us or our company? • Could this history be brought up in this meeting? If so, how will we address it?	

RELEVANT EXECUTIVE CALL PLAN, *continued*

Our Relationship with the *Relevant Executive*
- What actions has the *relevant executive* implemented or taken (toward us) to demonstrate this level of relationship?
- What actions can we now take to elevate our current level of business relationship?
- Have we/they promised any Action Items in any previous meetings that we need to address?
- What is our current level of relationship with the *relevant executive?*

Level of relationship:
Commodity Supplier—You are trying to make a sale. Your level of contribution to the client organization is minimal. Executives will typically send you down to lower levels in the organization.
Emerging Resource—You are beginning to make a contribution to the client's organization, however, your access to executives may still be limited.
Problem Solver—You are clearly making a difference in the client's organization, and they call you. You will typically now be granted access to certain executives on a regular basis.
Trusted Advisor—Your relationship becomes collaborative and you may be asked for advice on issues unrelated to your company's products or services.

RELEVANT EXECUTIVE CALL PLAN, *continued*

Past Value and Value We Will Deliver • What past value have we delivered to this organization? • To whom have we communicated our past value? When did that meeting take place? • What value can we deliver to executive(s) during this call? • Does our value proposition clearly contrast the current approach (or competing method) with our proposed solution *in terms they would understand*?	
DURING THE CALL	
Purpose and Objectives of Our Call • What is the purpose of the meeting (tactical goal) and what are the objectives (strategic goal) of our meeting? Has the *relevant executive* agreed to them? • What information or insight can we get only from this audience? • What information do we want to obtain or validate during our call with this audience? • What insight and knowledge about the client do we have that we want to bring to their attention on this call?	

RELEVANT EXECUTIVE CALL PLAN, *continued*

Agenda and Discussion Flow	Introduction
• How will we open the call? • What key agenda topics will we cover? • Who (on our team) has the responsibility to lead each part of the session? • Who and when will we deliver the "value" message we intend to provide? • Who will watch the timing to ensure that, if we are running late, we address the most important topics/requests? • What questions will we ask to foster the right level and focus in the discussion? • Are we hoping to get a referral from these executive(s) to another influential player in the organization? If so, who will we request? When—Which Executive?	*Refer to your initial telephone call with the executive.* • *Cite your past experience.* ***Issues & Implications*** • *Ask questions that confirm your level of preparation.* • *Discuss the issues and implications.* • *Confirm the importance of the breakthrough initiative.* ***Solution Options*** • *Explore potential solutions.* • *Develop a vision of the optimal solution.* • *Confirm the value of the solution.* ***Moving Forward*** • *Reconnect with the executive to secure return access.* • *Create an action plan that involves the executive.*
Closing • What progress must be demonstrated by the executive(s) (e.g., commitment to buy, introduction to new influencer or decision maker) in order for us to deem the call successful? • What specific actions will we ask the executive(s) to take? Who will be responsible for raising these actions? • Who is responsible for delivering the call summary and ensure that we have a strong closing?	

RELEVANT EXECUTIVE CALL PLAN, *continued*

AFTER THE CALL	
Actions • Did you appropriately thank the executive(s) who participated in the call (immediately after the session)? Did you also thank *your* company's executives and offer to update them on future progress with this client? • Did you properly set expectations and gain resolution on the issues you presented to the executives during the call? • What is the plan to reconnect with the *relevant executive* in a timely fashion to keep the momentum moving forward? • How should we work with other executive(s) in the client organization to advance our objectives? • Did we summarize all actions to ensure that all team members are briefed and owners are assigned?	

RELEVANT EXECUTIVE CALL PLAN—EXAMPLE

CLIENT	DATE OF INITIAL MEETING
Self Assembled Furniture (SAF)	5/20/20XX
NAME OF *RELEVANT EXECUTIVE*	**POSITION**
Ben Tan	Chief Financial Officer (CFO)
SALESPERSON NAME	**INITIAL SALES OPPORTUNITY**
Tim Burr	IT Systems Upgrade

Have we identified the relevant executive for the sales opportunity within this client organization? The relevant executive is defined as the executive who stands to gain the most or lose the most as a result of the application or project associated with our sales opportunity. Typically there is one relevant executive in the client organization for a specific sales opportunity; however, if you have multiple opportunities within the same organization, each opportunity may have a unique relevant executive.

PRIOR TO THE CALL

About the *Relevant Executive* and Client Organization

- Who have we identified as the *relevant executive* and what are his or her formal roles and responsibilities in the organization?
- How is he or she measured and rewarded?
- What decisions can this executive influence or make independently?
- Who is in his or her influence network?
- Whose influence network is he or she in?
- Does he or she have affiliations with other companies?
- Where was the executive hired from (previous companies—if applicable)?
- Who does the relevant executive report to and what is the relationship between those two individuals?

Ben Tan, CFO, is clearly the relevant executive at SAF International. He has been with SAF for 7 years and has had an impressive record of achievement over that time. For the project associated with our sales opportunity, Tan has the most to gain if the project goes well and the most to lose if the project fails.

Tan secured the funding for the project of concurrently revamping all three major product lines and is rumored to be the top candidate for the CEO position when the current CEO retires (within the next 2 years). As a result, it is thought that Tan can have a significant amount of informal influence over the selection of the vendor for the IT systems upgrade.

Tan reports to Miles Prower (CEO) who has been with SAF International for 8 years. Tan, who is known for his significant accomplishments as CFO at SAF, has a strong relationship with Prower who respects his financial expertise and abilities as a CFO.

RELEVANT EXECUTIVE CALL PLAN—EXAMPLE, *continued*

Business Pressures and Initiatives	
Business Pressures and Initiatives • What are the internal and external pressures driving the need for change (e.g., Financial, Operational, Competitive, Customer, Supplier, Business Partner, and the like)? • Which key business objective is most important to the relevant executive and why? • What are the plans or initiatives the client has put in place to address these significant business pressures? • Is the application or project associated with our sales opportunity linked with a key business initiative? • How could we make an impact on the client's business and/or help them address this key business initiative?	Several key business issues are facing SAF, namely: (1) Financial pressures—their pace of revenue growth is slowing and their rate of profitability has decreased. (2) Operational pressures—the viability of the current IT system is questionable, with respect to supporting the introduction of the three new product lines. (3) Competitive pressures—if the network infrastructure cannot support the expected increased demand for worldwide customer orders, it may reduce sales. It will also provide an opportunity for competitors to make gains. Additionally it may drive channel partners, which include retail outlets such as Office Depot and Staples to become more aggressive competitors, rather than partners. To address these pressures, SAF has implemented the key initiative of concurrently revamping their three major product lines. This will create an opportunity for us (Systemflex) to upgrade the existing IT infrastructure, at a cost of $700K.

RELEVANT EXECUTIVE CALL PLAN—EXAMPLE, *continued*

Known or Anticipated Obstacles • What obstacles are known or anticipated? From whom? Why? How can they be addressed and mitigated in advance? • Is there any history with this client that might impact their perceptions of us or our company? • Could this history be brought up in this meeting? If so, how will we address it?	Joe King, IT Director, is our main contact at SAF. He has been a key supporter of Systemflex, but over the years has made numerous modifications to the existing IT system. Some people on his team now feel that these modifications have significantly reduced the system throughput and degraded its performance. While that may be the case, King is adamant in his conclusion that the existing IT system will support the new product introductions because he can implement additional modifications to the system, if they are required. We suspect that King's reluctance to upgrade the system might be related to his upcoming retirement. King could be a major obstacle in us getting an appointment to meet with Tan; however, in the absence of that meeting, our chances of winning the deal are at risk. Theresa Green, CIO, seems to have an open mind. However, she is a conservative thinker, doesn't have the detailed technical knowledge of information systems, and tends to take a skeptical view of new technology, until pressed into action. You're beginning to think that she now concurs with King's assessment of the capabilities of the current system. While our past value to SAF has been significant, that value has never been communicated to any executives at SAF.

RELEVANT EXECUTIVE CALL PLAN—EXAMPLE, *continued*

Our Relationship with the *Relevant Executive*

- What actions have the *relevant executive* implemented or taken (toward us) to demonstrate this level of relationship?
- What actions can we now take to elevate our current level of business relationship?
- Have we/they promised any Action Items in any previous meetings that we need to address?
- What is our current level of relationship with the *relevant executive?*

Level of relationship:
Commodity Supplier—You are trying to make a sale. Your level of contribution to the client organization is minimal. Executives will typically send you down to lower levels in the organization.
Emerging Resource—You are beginning to make a contribution to the client's organization, however, your access to executives may still be limited.
Problem Solver—You are clearly making a difference in the client's organization, and they call you. You will typically now be granted access to certain executives on a regular basis.
Trusted Advisor—Your relationship becomes collaborative and you may be asked for advice on issues unrelated to your company's products or services.

While we have only had a brief introduction to Ben Tan, we have had in-depth meetings with key members of his staff over the past year. One of those meetings involved a comprehensive review of the capabilities of the existing IT systems, and several managers who reported to Tan came up to you after the review to comment on your professionalism, as well as your thorough approach.

We should try to leverage those relationships (with members of Tan's staff) to gain access to Tan. Specifically, we could ask one of Tan's managers to provide us with a formal introduction to Tan.

Overall, our level of business relationship could be viewed as that of a Problem Solver, because we have a comprehensive understanding of SAF's business and their key customers, as well as their competitors.

In addition, we bring a unique perspective of understanding not only the capabilities of the existing IT system, but the enhancements that would be required of the new IT system to make it immediately viable (so that it could support the introduction of the three new product lines).

Our proposed solution also minimizes the switching costs, while providing continued value to SAF. We should also make this point to our primary sponsor, Joe King, because the switch (from our existing IT system to any of our competitors) would be substantial, something which King would probably rather avoid.

RELEVANT EXECUTIVE CALL PLAN—EXAMPLE, *continued*

Past Value and Value We Will Deliver • What past value have we delivered to this organization? • To whom have we communicated our past value? When did that meeting take place? • What value can we deliver to executive(s) during this call? • Does our value proposition clearly contrast the current approach (or competing method) with our proposed solution *in terms they would understand*?	While our past value to SAF has been significant, that value has never been communicated to any executives at SAF (including Tan). We should clearly take advantage of our initial meeting with Tan to communicate the past value we have delivered to SAF, as well as our commitment to continuing to deliver value in the future.
DURING THE CALL	
Purpose and Objectives of Our Call • What is the purpose of the meeting (tactical goal) and what are the objectives (strategic goal) of our meeting? Has the *relevant executive* agreed to them? • What information or insight can we get only from this audience? • What information do we want to obtain or validate during our call with this audience? • What insight and knowledge about the client do we have that we want to bring to their attention on this call?	The main purpose of the initial face-to-face meeting on Ben Tan is to make certain that Tan is aware that Systemflex has viable solution options to offer SAF, as they move ahead with the revamping of their three major product lines. As part of this meeting, we want Tan to validate the importance of the successful product introductions not only as a breakthrough initiative for SAF, but as being personally important to him.

RELEVANT EXECUTIVE CALL PLAN—EXAMPLE, *continued*

Agenda and Discussion Flow	Overall Agenda
• How will we open the call? • What key agenda topics will we cover? • Who (on our team) has the responsibility to lead each part of the session? • Who and when will we deliver the "value" message we intend to provide? • Who will watch the timing to ensure that if we are running late we address the most important topics/requests? • What questions will we ask to foster the right level and focus in the discussion? • Are we hoping to get a referral from these executive(s) to another influential player in the organization? If so, who will we request? When—Which Executive?	• Introduction • Refer to our sponsor who provided the introduction to Tan Issues & Implications • Ask questions that demonstrate our level of preparation and our knowledge and understanding of SAF's business, as well as SAF's key business initiatives and business drivers Solution Options • Explore potential solution options and verify Tan's opinion regarding the current IT system and its capabilities. In addition, get Tan's view of a successful outcome of the project Moving Forward • Develop a plan to reconnect with Tan, assuring return access • Tim Burr will open the meeting and rely on one of his associates to watch the timing of the content

RELEVANT EXECUTIVE CALL PLAN—EXAMPLE, *continued*

Closing	Our main objective is to get Tan to commit to one (or more) of the following:
• What progress must be demonstrated by the executive(s) (e.g., commitment to buy, introduction to new influencer or decision maker) in order for us to deem the call as being successful?	• A follow-on meeting with Systemflex where Tan is directly involved
• What specific actions will we ask the executive(s) to take? Who will be responsible to raise these actions?	• A commitment from Tan to have his staff take the next steps with Systemflex to develop an implementation plan for the IT system upgrade, combined with Tan's agreement to review that plan with us
• Who is responsible for delivering the call summary and ensure that we have a strong closing?	Tim Burr is responsible for summarizing the meeting at the end of the face-to-face call with Tan—ensuring that Systemflex has a strong closing. It is also Tim's responsibility to distribute copies of the call summary to all of Systemflex's participants within 2 business days of the meeting.

RELEVANT EXECUTIVE CALL PLAN—EXAMPLE, *continued*

AFTER THE CALL	
Actions • Did you appropriately thank the executive(s) who participated in the call (immediately after the session)? Did you also thank *your* company's executives and offer to update them on future progress with this client? • Did you properly set expectations and gain resolution on the issues you presented to the executives during the call? • What is the plan to reconnect with the *relevant executive* in a timely fashion to keep the momentum moving forward? • How should we work with other executive(s) in the client organization to advance our objectives? • Did we summarize all actions to ensure that all team members are briefed and owners are assigned?	• Tim Burr should ensure that Tan and his staff, as well as the executives from Systemflex, have received appropriate thank you notes for their involvement in the session • The entire Systemflex team should meet and review the call within 48 hours of the session to make certain that the expectations of the call with Tan were met • Tim Burr should ensure that Systemflex has the right plans in place to reconnect with each of the executives from SAF. It might be appropriate for certain Systemflex executives to follow-up with executives from SAF who they personally connected with during the meeting • Tim Burr should ensure that we have plans in place to reconnect with the appropriate executives from SAF • Tim Burr has the responsibility to follow-up with all members of Systemflex who participated in the session to make certain they were each briefed on the outcome of the call and they fully understand their roles in the next steps

Recommended Reading

Visit any physical or online bookstore and you'll find thousands of books related to sales, marketing, management strategy, and global perspectives. Some of them are better than others. The following have helped us on our journey.

On Selling

Lee Bartlett, *The No. 1 Bestseller,* London: Lee Bartlett, 2016.

Jeb Blount, *Sales EQ,* Hoboken, NJ: John Wiley & Sons, 2017.

Michael Bowland and Keith Hawk, *Get-Real Selling,* Belgium: Nova Vista Publishing, 2008.

Anthony Iannarino, *The Only Sales Guide You'll Ever Need,* New York: Portfolio Penguin, 2016.

John P. Kotter, *Power and Influence: Beyond Formal Authority,* New York: Free Press, 1985.

David H. Maister, Charles H. Green, and Robert M. Galford, *The Trusted Advisor,* New York: Free Press, 2000.

Rick Page, *Hope Is Not a Strategy: The 6 Keys to Winning the Complex Sale,* New York: Nautilus Press, 2002.

Neil Rackham and John Devincentis, *Rethinking the Sales Force: Redefining Selling to Create and Capture Customer Value*, New York: McGraw-Hill, 1999.

Neil Rackham, *SPIN Selling*, New York: McGraw-Hill, 1988.

Nicholas A. C. Read, *Target Opportunity Selling: Top Sales Performers Reveal What Really Works*, New York: McGraw-Hill, 2013.

Jagdish Sheth and Andrew Sobel, *Clients for Life: How Great Professionals Develop Breakthrough Relationships*, New York: Simon & Schuster, 2000.

Andrew Sobel, *All for One: 10 Strategies for Building Trusted Client Partnerships*, Hoboken, NJ: John Wiley & Sons, 2009.

Duane Sparks, *Action Selling*, Minneapolis: The Sales Board Inc., 2004.

Jerry Stapleton, *From Vendor to Business Resource*, Fort Collins, CO: Summa Business Books, 2002.

Dave Stein, *How Winners Sell*, Austin: Bard Press, 2002.

Tom Stevenson and Sam Barcus, *The Relationship Advantage—Become a Trusted Advisor and Create Clients for Life*, Chicago: Dearborn Trade Publishing, 2003.

On Marketing

Malcolm Gladwell, *The Tipping Point: How Little Things Can Make a Big Difference*, Boston: Little Brown, 2000.

Hugh Macfarlane, *The Leaky Funnel*, 2d ed., South Melbourne: MathMarketing, 2007.

Mary A. Molloy and Michael K. Molloy, *The Buck Starts Here: Profit-Based Sales & Marketing Made Easy*, Cincinnati, OH: Thomson Executive Press, 1996.

Geoffrey A. Moore, *Crossing the Chasm: Marketing and Selling Technology Products to Mainstream Customers*, New York: HarperCollins, 1991.

Geoffrey A. Moore, *Inside the Tornado: Strategies for Developing, Leveraging, and Surviving Hypergrowth Markets*, New York: Collins Business, 2004.

Emanuel Rosen, *The Anatomy of Buzz: How to Create Word of Mouth Marketing*, New York: Doubleday Business, 2002.

Robert J. Schmonsees, *Escaping the Black Hole: Minimizing the Damage from the Marketing-Sales Disconnect*, Mason, OH: Southwestern Educational Publishing, 2005.

Dan Stiff, *Sell the Brand First: How to Sell Your Brand and Create Lasting Customer Loyalty*, New York: McGraw-Hill, 2006.

On Management

Kenneth Blanchard and Spencer Johnson, *The New One Minute Manager*, London: Thorsons Harper Collins, 2015.

Bob Gates, *A Passion for Leadership: Lessons on Change and Reform from Fifty Years of Public Service*, New York: Knopf, 2016.

Louis V. Gerstner, Jr., *Who Says Elephants Can't Dance: Inside IBM's Historic Turnaround*, New York: Harper Collins, 2002.

W. Chan Kim and Renee Mauborgne, *Blue Ocean Strategy*, Expanded Edition, Boston: Harvard Business School Publishing, 2015.

L. David Marquet, *Turn the Ship Around!: A True Story of Building Leaders by Breaking the Rules*, Austin: Portfolio Penguin, 2015.

Michael E. Porter, *Competitive Strategy*, New York: Free Press, 2004.

Simon Sinek, *Start With Why: How Great Leaders Inspire Everyone to Take Action*, London: Penguin Books, 2011.

David G. Thomson, *Blueprint to a Billion*, New York: John Wiley & Sons, 2006.

Jack Welch and John A. Byrne, *Jack: Straight From the Gut*, New York: Grand Central Publishing, 2003.

On Personal Professionalism

Dale Carnegie, *How to Win Friends and Influence People*, New York: Pocket Books, 1988.

Stephen R. Covey, *The 7 Habits of Highly Effective People*, New York: Free Press, 2004.

Timothy Ferriss, *The 4-Hour Work Week*, New York: Crown Publishers, 2007.

Raymond M. Kethledge and Michael S. Erwin, *Lead Yourself First: Inspiring Leadership Through Solitude*, New York: Bloomsbury Publishing, 2017.

David H. Maister, *True Professionalism*, New York: Free Press, 1997.

Og Mandino, *The Greatest Salesman in the World*, Hollywood: Bantam, 1995.

Anthony Robbins, *Awaken the Giant Within*, New York: Free Press, 1992.

On Western Business Strategy

Baron Carl von Clausewitz, *On War*, New York: Oxford University Press, 2007.

Donald G. Krause, *The Art of War for Executives: Ancient Knowledge for Today's Business Professional*, New York: Perigee, 2007.

Niccolò Machiavelli, *The Prince*, New York: Bantam Classics, 1984.

U.S. Army with an Introduction by General David H. Petraeus, Lt. General James F. Amos, and Lt. Colonel John A. Nagl, *The U.S. Army/ Marine Corps Counterinsurgency Field Manual*, Chicago: University of Chicago Press, 2007.

On Eastern Business Strategy

Chin-Ning Chu, *Thick Face, Black Heart: The Warrior Philosophy for Conquering the Challenges of Business and Life*, New York: Business Plus, 1998.

Ted Fishman, *China, Inc.*, New York: Scribner, 2005.

Kaihan Krippendorff, *Hide a Dagger Behind a Smile: Use the 36 Ancient Chinese Strategies to Seize the Competitive Edge*, Avon, MA: Adams Media, 2008.

Miyamoto Musashi, *The Book of Five Rings*, New York: Shambhala, 2005.

Sun Tzu, *The Art of War*, with a Foreword by James Clavell. New York: Delta, 1989.

On Global Perspective

Gary Allen and Larry Abraham, *None Dare Call It Conspiracy*, revised edition, Cutchogue, NY: Buccaneer Books, 1982.

Jared Diamond, *Guns, Germs and Steel: The Fates of Human Societies*, 20th Anniversary Edition, New York: W. W. Norton and Company, 2017.

Daniel Estulin, *The True Story of the Bilderberg Group*, Waterville, OR: TrineDay, 2007.

Thomas L. Friedman, *Thank You for Being Late: An Optimist's Guide to Thriving in the Age of Acceleration*, New York: Farrar, Straus and Giroux, 2016.

Thomas L. Friedman, *The World Is Flat: A Brief History of the Twenty-First Century*, New York: Farrar, Straus and Giroux, 2005.

Gavin Menzies, *1421: The Year China Discovered America*, New York: HarperCollins, 2003.

Condoleezza Rice, *Democracy: Stories from the Long Road to Freedom*, New York: Grand Central Publishing, 2017.

James Surowiecki, *The Wisdom of Crowds*, New York: Anchor, 2005.

Don Tapscott and Anthony D. Williams, *Wikinomics: How Mass Collaboration Change Everything*, expanded edition, New York: Portfolio Hardcover, 2008.

Fareed Zakaria, *The Post-American World*, New York: W. W. Norton and Company, 2008.

Recommended Associations
and Organizations

You need a license to drive a car or an aircraft, a certificate to fix pipes or wires, and a degree to practice engineering or law. Yet there is no formal accreditation for the profession of selling, despite the fact that it plays a mission-critical role in business.

Selling requires its practitioners to be responsible for projecting complex financial calculations worthy of any accountant; for high-stakes negotiations worthy of any statesman; for designing elegant solutions worthy of any architect; for delivering presentations worthy of any advertising director; for exercising competitive savvy worthy of any strategist; for demonstrating leadership under pressure worthy of any general; for preserving customer confidences worthy of any priest; for helping customers find their own answers worthy of any psychologist; for packaging visual and narrative information worthy of any producer; for educating customers worthy of any teacher.

We could go on, but you get the point. Selling is many roles rolled into one. Yet educational institutions have largely ignored the profession. It would be polite to say that the universities don't know how to classify such a diverse role. But the truth is that most of them simply don't see sales as a profession with standards and disciplines that can be taught and measured. If marketing is criticized as being the domain of *breakfasts and brochures*, sales is known for *lunches and lattes*. It took until 2002 for such stereotypes to be overcome and for standards to be drafted for teaching professional selling at the university level.

We list here some of the more prominent associations promoting this movement, plus some of the better magazines and journals in the market.

STRATEGIC ACCOUNT MANAGEMENT ASSOCIATION

Founded in 1964, the Strategic Account Management Association (SAMA) focuses on helping establish strategic, key, and global account management as a separate profession, career path, and proven corporate strategy for growth. SAMA is a nonprofit association with more than 8,000 members worldwide offering training, professional development, and networking events in North America, Asia, and Europe each year, in addition to research, publications, and other knowledge resources.

http://www.strategicaccounts.org/

THE SALES ASSOCIATION

The Sales Association is a professional society dedicated specifically to sales and business development professionals. Its mission is to connect its members with the professional sales community, providing them with a variety of offerings such as webinars and other local events. Monthly webinars are available on a range of subjects relevant to the sales professional.

http://www.salesassociation.org/

ASSOCIATION OF PROFESSIONAL SALES

Founded in 2014, the Association of Professional Sales (APS) in England is a nonprofit membership-based body that seeks to raise the credibility of sales practitioners. It does this by representing the sales profession to government departments, schools, businesses, and consumers as a role that holds itself to ethical and commercial standards, and which presents a viable career option to school leavers. To this end, it has pursued government endorsement of a sales apprenticeship program and provides various thought leadership publications and activities to its members.

https://associationofprofessionalsales.com

UNIVERSITY SALES CENTER ALLIANCE

Formed in 2002, the University Sales Center Alliance (USCA) is an organization that helps universities promote selling to students as a viable career option by sharing information on how to establish the academic stream and then assisting in the sharing of best practices for curriculum development, intercollegiate sales competitions, placement of graduates, and other related consulting activities. Its website lists universities that teach Sales as a degree program.

http://www.universitysalescenteralliance.org/

NATIONAL COLLEGIATE SALES COMPETITION

The National Collegiate Sales Competition (NCSC) was launched to promote the sales profession as an attractive career choice by providing a forum where students enrolled in a certified sales degree program could compete and exhibit their skills against national rival schools, and provide corporate sponsors with an opportunity to preview students for their recruitment pool. Its website lists universities that teach Sales as a degree program.

https://www.ncsc-ksu.org/

SELLING POWER

Selling Power magazine provides sales managers with content delivered through print, audio, video, and webinars. It also runs a Sales Leadership Conference series of speakers offering best practices, tactical solutions, and proven strategies to help sales leaders create more efficient and effective sales organizations.

http://www.sellingpower.com/

SALES AND MARKETING MANAGEMENT

Sales and Marketing Management (SMM) provides a wide array of print and digital resources for sales managers and sales professionals. Its monthly magazine is archived and available online. In addition to articles and white papers, SMM offers monthly webinars on a range of issues relevant to sales managers. Webinars are archived and available for viewing online.

https://salesandmarketing.com/

THE INTERNATIONAL JOURNAL OF SALES TRANSFORMATION

The *International Journal of Sales Transformation* is a UK-based magazine for the promotion of sales excellence among global corporates. Its subscribers are sales leaders, sales performance specialists, CEOs, and academics with an interest in sales strategy, talent, and execution. Its articles focus on complex sales and transactional selling at scale.

http://www.journalofsalestransformation.com

Notes

Preface

1 Priit Kallas, "Top 15 Most Popular Social Networking Sites and Apps," September 5, 2017, https://www.dreamgrow.com/top-15-most-popular -social-networking-sites/.

2 BNP Paribas, "2016 BNP Paribas Global Entrepreneur Report."

3 Kate Palmer, "Record 80 New Companies Being Born an Hour in 2016," *The Telegraph,* July 12, 2016.

Chapter 1

1 Elaine Wong, "The Most Memorable Product Launches of 2010," *Forbes*, December 2010.

2 Sara Radicati, "2015-2019 Email Statistics Report," The Radicati Group, March 2015.

3 Schneider Associates and Sentient Decision Science, "15th Annual 2016 Most Memorable New Product Launch Survey," March 2016.

Chapter 2

1 Kathleen Schaub, "Social Buying Meets Social Selling," IDC, April 2014.

2   David Weinhaus, "Sales Enablement Services to Drive Client Results and Boost Agency Fees," Hubspot, 2015, and Ryan Gum, "How to Use Sales Productivity to Sell Smarter, backed by Data," Attach, 2016.

3   "Making the Consensus Sale," Harvard Business Review, March 2015.

4   Hank Barbes, "In Enterprise Tech, Sell Broadly (Within an Account) Is the Only Answer," Gartner Group, 2016.

5   SalesLabs, "The Million Minute Sales Truth," Dialogue Review, April 2017.

6   "The Ultimate Contact Strategy," Velocify, 2013.

7   Interview with Neil Rackham by Josh Krist, a content manager for SalesLobby, a sales resource website operated by the Alexander Group Inc., September 2000. See also http://www.saleslobby.com/Online Magazine/0900/features_NRackham.asp.

8   Dave Chaffey, E-mail marketing statistics 2017, Smart Insights, June 2017.

9   Kath Pay, "The State of the Email Marketing By Industry," GetResponse, January 2016.

10   Kissmetrics, "The Growth Marketers Guide to Customer Engagement Automation," 2017.

11   Jakob Nielsen, "How Long Do Users Stay on Web Pages?," Nielsen Norman Group, September 2011.

12   Kissmetrics, "The Growth Marketers Guide to Customer Engagement Automation," 2017.

13   Ethan Denney, "The 4-Step Process for Converting Website Visitors into Potential Clients for Your Services," ConvertFlow, 2015.

14   Ibid.

15   Ibid.

16   Ibid.

Chapter 3

1   Rachel Gillett, "The Best and Worst Times to Post on Social Media," Fast Company, September 25, 2014.

2 "The Million Minute Sales Truth," *Dialogue Review*, April 19, 2017.

3 *Journal of Air Transport Management* 10, no. 1 (January 2004).

4 Kristin Rivera and Per-Ola Karlsson, "CEOs Are Getting Fired for Ethical Lapses More Than They Used To," *Harvard Business Review*, 6 June 2017.

5 Elliott Haworth, "One Year Until the EU General Data Protection Regulation," CityAM, May 24, 2017.

6 Doug Drinkwater, "These CISOs Explain Why They Got Fired," *CSO Magazine*, April 20, 2016.

Chapter 4

1 Louis V. Gerstner, Jr., *Who Says Elephants Can't Dance: Inside IBM's Historic Turnaround*, HarperBusiness, 2002.

2 Doug Garr, *IBM Redux: Lou Gerstner and the Business Turnaround of the Decade*, HarperBusiness, 1999.

3 United Nations press release SG/SM/6161, February 19, 1997.

4 Joshua Green, "Karl Rove in a Corner," *Atlantic Monthly*, November, 2004.

5 James Moore and Wayne Slater, *"Bush's Brain: How Karl Rove Made George W. Bush Presidential,"* New York: John Wiley & Sons, 2003.

Chapter 5

1 http://www.cbbc.org/mic2025/.

2 Wade Shepard, "China Hits Record High M&A Investments in Western Firms," *Forbes*, September 10, 2016.

3 Target Opportunity Planning Sales Performance Index, SalesLabs, 2017.

Chapter 6

1 Of this number, 14.4 percent were in the process of quitting or onboarding, 44.4 percent were looking for new opportunities with

updated résumés, and 30.6 percent indicated an intention to switch jobs. Only 10.6 percent would not consider job-searching. Source: HR in Asia, November 1, 2016.

2 Sarang Sunder, V. Kumar, Ashley Goreczny, and Todd Maurer, "How to Predict Turnover on Your Sales Team," *Harvard Business Review*, August 2017. Based on research in "Why Do Salespeople Quit? An Empirical Examination of Own and Peer Effects on Salesperson Turnover Behavior," *Journal of Marketing Research*, 2016.

Chapter 7

1 Encarta.msn.com/dictionary_/proposition.html.

2 "The Oil Sands of Alberta," *60 Minutes*, CBS. Originally aired January 22, 2006.

Chapter 8

1 Jennifer Polk, "Differentiate Digital Commerce With Customer Experience," Gartner, May 21, 2016.

2 Michael Krigsman, "Brand Promise, Customer Experience, and CMO Lessons for the CIO," ZDNet, 2017.

3 "Omni Channel Customer Experience: Not an Option, But a Strategic Necessity," Frost & Sullivan, 2016.

Index

Page numbers followed by *f* indicate figures.

A

ABC, 22
AC Milan, 104
Access, gaining. *See* Gaining executive access
Advertising, 5, 31, 35, 64, 137
Alberta, Canada, 165
Alibaba, 4
All for One: 10 Strategies for Building Trusted Client Partnerships (Sobel), 175
Amazon, 4
AMC Theatres, 104
Anbang Insurance, 104
Annan, Kofi, 92
Approach, initial, 111–116
Approvers, 82–83
Ask.fm, xvii
Association of Professional Sales (APS), 249
Aston Villa, 104
Atlantic magazine, 92
Australia, 10

B

B2B selling, 31, 182
Baby boomers, 5
Bain & Co., 172
Beech, Hannah, 105
Beijing, China, 22
Beijing Olympics, 105
Benefits, expected *vs.* delivered, 121, 122, 122*f*
Bezos, Jeff, 105
Bistritz, Steve, 6
Blogs, 30, 57, xvii
Borders, 3
Breakthrough initiatives, 146

Bush, George H.W., 92
Bush, George W., 92–93
Business drivers, 124
Business Issues Worksheet, 219
Business partner drivers, 69–70
Business Process Reengineering, 2
Business value, specific, 158
Buyer's journey, 35–36, 39, 120–121
Buying cycle, 10–16
Buying decisions, 82

C

Cadence, in e-mail marketing, 43–44
Camp David, 93
Campaign Monitor, 42
Canada, 64
Capability, 126, 127, 127*f*, 153, 158
CEB Inc., 37
Center for Business & Industrial Marketing, 8, xii
Cerutti, 104
Chats, 47
ChemChina, 104
Chevrolet, 72
Chiang Kai-shek, 103
China
    Coca-Cola in, 72
    Dèng Xiǎopíng and, 91–92
    Executive MBA programs for executives in, 9–10
    importance of communicating value in, 139, 140
    importance of knowledge of industry/ company in, 135–136

China, *continued*
  as low-cost provider, 2
  mindset of executives in, 101–106, 132
Click-Through Rate (CTR), 40, 43
Click-to-Open Rate (CTOR), 40–43, 42*f*
Client loyalty, 172–187
  building, 175, 177
  cultivating, 176–187
Client Value Zone, 127, 130, 195
Club Med, 104
Coca-Cola, 72
Commodity Supplier(s), 16–20, 63, 149, 164, 185
Common ground, exploring, 177–179
Communication
  consistency in, 181, 195–196
  and formal value review, 165–166
  as foundation for client loyalty, 174–175
  and overcommunicating, 180
  and past value, 107, 230, 237
  routing, 28
  and undercommunicating, 180
  of value, 38–40, 138–140, 181
Company resources, value of, 154*f*, 155–156
Company solutions, value of, 154*f*, 156
Compaq, 3
Competitor drivers, 71
Consultative-type questions, 133–134
ConvertFlow, 47
Credibility, 101, 115–116, 147, 148
  building, 122–126, 129–131
  components of, 126, 127*f*
  criteria for establishing, 133
  establishing, with executives, 124–125
  executive's perception of salesperson's, 123
CTOR (Click-to-Open Rate), 40–43, 42*f*
CTR (Click-Through Rate), 40, 43
Customer drivers, 70–71
Customer experience contact preferences, 183*f*
Customer-focused value proposition, 159*f*, 161*f*, 162

D

Decision makers, 82
Decision making. *See* Executive decision making
Decision-making process, 82, 133
Delivered benefits, 121, 122, 122*f*
Dell, 3, 4
Dèng Xiǎopíng, 91–92, 104
Denney, Ethan, 47
Dialogue Review, 64–65
Direct sales force, 2
Dirt Devil, 104
Door Closers, 34–35, 35*f*
Door Openers, 34–36, 35*f*
DTMF IVR, 183

E

EBay, 4
Ebersol, Dick, 22–23
Economy, viii

Econsultancy, 47
Electrolux, 32, 33*f*
E-mail, 5, 183, xvii
E-mail campaign pages, 44–49
E-mail marketing, 35–36, 40–44, 46
E-mail open rate, 41*f*
Emerging Resources, 18–19, 127, 149, 185
Empirical research, xii
England, 64
Executive decision making
  business partner drivers and, 69–70
  competitor drivers and, 71
  customer drivers and, 70–71
  drivers of, 66–74, 66*f*
  financial drivers and, 67–68
  globalization drivers and, 71–72
  operational drivers and, 68
  regulatory drivers and, 72–73
  supplier drivers and, 68–69
Executive Presentation Guide, 222–226
Executive-Level Meeting Planner (form), 220
Executives
  benefits delivered to, 121–122, 122*f*
  establishing credibility with (*See* Credibility)
  expectations of salespeople and, 123*f*
  expected benefits of, 121–122, 122*f*
  first meeting with, 131*f*
  involvement of, in buying cycle, 10–16
  role-specific issues of, 74*f*
  understanding needs of, 55–60
Expected benefits, 121, 122, 122*f*

F

Facebook, 57, 106, 183, xvii
Federal Express, 3
Financial drivers, 67–68
Fiverr, 36
Flickr, xvii
Flynn, Gillian, 137
Follow-on meetings, 148–150
For the Record: From Wall Street to Washington (Regan), 91
Forbes, 5
Ford Motor Company, 72
Formal value reviews, 165–167
Fortis Insurance, 104
1421: The Year China Discovered America (Menzies), 101
Fox, 22
France, 65
Freelancer.com, 36
Friedman, Thomas, 3, 30
Frost & Sullivan, 182

G

Gaining executive access, 100–116, 109*f*
  and commitment to action, 113–116
  and credibility of salesperson, 113
  initial contact, 111–116

introduction, 112–113
preparation, 112
purpose of call, 113
Game, getting in the, 55–58
Gartner, Inc., 37, 182
Gatekeeper approach, to gaining executive access, 109f, 110–111
Gatekeepers, 107–108
GDPR (General Data Protection Regulation), 73
GE Appliances, 104
Gen X, 5, 59
Gen Y (millennials), 5, 59
Gen Z, 5, 59
General Data Protection Regulation (GDPR), 73
General Electric, 18
Generation Y, 182, xviii
Generation Z, 182
Georgia State University, 8, xii
Germany, 65
Gerstner, Lou, 85
GetResponse, 40, 43
Gieves & Hawkes Tailors of London, 104
Globalization drivers, 71–72
Goldman Sachs, 3
Gone Girl (Flynn), 137
Google, 63
Google+, xvii
GoToMeeting, 183
Grindr, 104
Guanxi, 105–106, 132, 140
Guanxi and Business (Luo Yadong), 89
Guide to Client Discovery, 61, 178, 200–213
and information on client executive, 203–204, 211
and information on client's company, 202–203, 212
and information on client's industry, 201–202, 211
periodicals and news services, 205–206
and preparing for initial meeting, 210
search engines, 204–205
sources of information, 207–208
Gulf War, 92–93

H

Harvey Nichols, 104
Hewlett-Packard (HP), 6–9, ix, xii
Hewlett-Packard Business School (Beijing), 9, xii
Hong Kong, 102
Hoover, 104
House of Fraser, 104
Human agent, 183

I

IBM, 40, 85–86, 104, 128–129
IDC, 29
India, 2
Indonesia, 10
Industrial Revolution, 102
Influence, 92–94. *See also* Organizational influence
effects of, 94–95

gaining, 86–87
losing, 86–87
and network, 101
situational, 96
Information monopolies, 30
Ingram Micro, 104
Initial Executive Telephone Call Planner (form), 217
Inner circle, 95–96, 95f, 101
Instagram, xvii
Integrity, 126, 127, 127f
Inter Milan, 104
International Journal of Sales Transformation, 250
International Olympic Committee (IOC), 23
Internet, 4, 14, 30–31
Introduction stage (of meetings), 146
Ironman, 104
Irrelevant executives, 84
Issues and implications stage (of meetings), 146–147
IWG plc, 48–49

J

Jackson, Janet, 87
Japan, 10

K

Kellogg School of Management, 47
Kenan-Flagler School of Business, 6, xii
Kissmetrics, 44, 46–47
Klompmaker, Jay, 7
Kodak, 3

L

Las Vegas, Nevada, 105
Leads, 15–16, 36–38, 44, 47, 51, 73, 109
Leaky Funnel, The (Macfarlane), 39
Lexus and the Olive Tree, The (Friedman), 3, 30
LinkedIn, 57, 106, 177–178, 183, xvii–xviii
London Taxis, 104
Low prices, 2
Loyalty. *See* Client loyalty
Loyalty Effect, The: The Hidden Force Behind Growth, Profits, and Lasting Value (Reichheld), 172–173
Loyalty Staircase, 177, 177f, 186
Luo Yadong, 89

M

Macfarlane, Hugh, 39
MailChimp, 40, 42
Malaysia, 10
Maney, Kevin, 30
Mao Zedong, 103
Marconi, 104
Marketing
development of modern, 31
e-mail, 35–36, 40–44, 46, xvii
Internet, 14, 30–31
and lead generation, 15–16, 36–38
and meetings, 12

Marketing, *continued*
  multichannel, 2
  and personal preferences, 31–33
  resources on, 242–243
  three-step model, 34–36, 35*f*
  by top sellers, 57
Marketing activities, 34
Marketing materials, 86
Marketing teams, 13
Mayer, Marissa, 73
Maytag, 104
Meeting(s), 145–150, 145*f*
  conducting an effective first, 194–195
  demonstrating integrity/capability in
      subsequent, 195
  introduction stage of, 146
  issues/implications stage of, 146–147
  moving forward stage of, 148–150
  research before initial, 194
  solution options stage of, 148
Menzies, Gavin, 101
Mergermarket Group, 104
MG Rover, 104
Microsoft Research, 45
Millenipreneurs, xviii
Millennials, 5, 59
Mindset, of Chinese executives, 101–106
Morgan Stanley, 104
Most Memorable New Product Launch, 5
Motorola, 104
Moving forward stage (of meetings), 148–150
Multichannel marketing, 2

N

National Collegiate Sales Competition (NCSC),
    249
NBC, 22
Needs of executives, understanding, 55–60
Network(s), 88–90, 95*f*, 96
  of advisors, 114
  personal, 115
New products, 2
New York City, 137
New York Times, 30
New Zealand, 90
Nielsen Norman Group, 45

O

Oldroyd, James, 47
Olympic Games, 22–23
Online web conferencing, 183
Open Rate (OR), 40, 41, 41*f*
Operational drivers, 68
Organizational influence, 86–96
  and degrees of influence, 93–94
  dynamics of, 86–96
  evaluating past performance, 87–88
  and executive's network, 88–90
  and exertion of will, 90–91
  and identifying the relevant executive, 88
  and value, 88

Overt approach, to gaining executive access,
    109, 109*f*

P

Page-visit durations, 45
Path, navigating a, 108–111
Patterns of success, 88
Pay, Kath, 43
Personal value, 154, 154*f*, 155
Personalization, 184
Perspectives, of stakeholders, 139*f*
Petro-Kazakhstan, 104
Philippines, 10
Pinterest, xvii
Pirelli, 104
Pizza Express, 104
Pop-up windows, 47, 48
Powell, Colin, 92
Print advertising, 5
Problem Solvers, 19–20, 126, 149, 150, 185
Product differentiation, 2
Product launches, 5
Product Vendor level of sales proficiency, 74
Prospects, 14, 31, 34–36, 35*f*, 41, 46, 48
Pudong New Area (China), 92
Purchasing decisions, 29, 29*f*, 30

Q

Qingdao Haier, 104
Questions
  asking, 60–61
  consultative-type, 133–134
  layers of, 144
  strategic, 146–147
Quigley, Joan, 91

R

Rackham, Neil, 38–39
Reagan, Nancy, 91
Reagan, Ronald, 91, 92
Recommendations, 100*f*
Reddit, xvii
Referral approach, to gaining executive access,
    109*f*, 110
Referrals, 100, 114, 115
Regan, Donald T., 91
Regulatory drivers, 72–73
Reichheld, Frederick, F., 172–173
Relevant executive(s), xv–xvi
  access to, 84, 107–108
  and credibility gap, 126
  customer-focused value proposition for, 162
  defining the, 82, 95*f*
  determining best approach to get to, 193–194
  identifying the, 81–82, 87, 193
  and inner circle, 95–96, 95*f*
  network of, 89–90
  perspective of, 150
Relevant Executive Call Plan (form), 227–240
Requests for proposal (RFPs), 28
Research, 59–65

and asking questions, 60–61
scheduling your, 59–60
value of, 61–65
Resources, 241–245
  on Eastern business strategy, 244
  on global perspective, 244–245
  on management, 243
  on marketing, 242–243
  on personal professionalism, 243–244
  on selling, 241–242
  on Western business strategy, 244
Response times, 47
Rethinking the Sales Force (Rackham and
  DeVincentis), 38
Revolving Door, 34–35, 35*f*
Rice, Condoleezza, 93
Rio Tinto, 104
RJR Nabisco, 85
Roadblock Worksheet, 218
Roadblocks, 106–108, 107*f*
Rondeau, Justin, 47
Rotary, 104
Routine, adopting a, 59–60
Rove, Karl, 92

S

Sales and Marketing Management (SMM), 250
Sales Association, 248
Sales Opportunity Profile (form), 216
Sales proficiency
  Commodity Supplier stage of, 16–18
  Emerging Resource stage of, 18–19
  Problem Solver stage of, 19–20
  stages of, 16*f*
  Trusted Advisor stage of, 20–23
SalesLabs, 9
SalesLobby.com, 38–39
Salespeople, 2–3
  ability of, to communicate value, 137–140
  ability of, to listen before prescribing solution,
    133–134
  ability of, to marshal resources, 124
  ability of, to solve problems, 137–138
  demonstrated accountability of, 132
  executive's perception of credibility in, 123
  and knowledge of industry/company, 135–137
  responsiveness of, to requests, 125
  understanding by, of goals/objectives of
    executives, 124–125, 133
  as value creators, x
  willingness of, to be held accountable,
    125–126, 132
Salt Lake City, Utah, 22, 79
San Diego, California, 79
Sandro, 104
Sarbanes-Oxley Act, 73
Saudi Arabia, 165
Schneider Associates, 5
Scotland, 64
Search engines, 5, 30
Seattle, Washington, 79

Selling Power magazine, 250
Sentient Decision Science, 5
Shanghai, China, 92
Shanghai World Expo, 105
Silk Road, 102
Silverpop, 40
Singapore, 10
Six Sigma, 2, 68
Skype, 183
Small and medium-size enterprises (SMEs), xv
Smart Insights, 40, 42
Smithfield Foods, 104
SMM (Sales and Marketing Management), 250
Sobel, Andrew, 175
Social media, 5, 29, xvii–xviii
Social networks, 30
Social proof, 30
Solution options stage (of meetings), 148
Solutions, 137–138, xvi
Sony, 3
South Korea, 10
Specific business value, 157, 157*f*, 158
Speech IVR, 183
SPIN Selling (Rackham), 38
Sponsor approach, to gaining executive access,
  109–110, 109*f*
Sports Illustrated, 22
Stakeholders
  and communicating value, 196
  creating value for, 88
  customer-focused value proposition for, 162
  influence of, 86–87, 93, 150
  meetings with various, 28
  and network building, 91
  perspectives of, 139*f*
  and relationship building, 38
  and value proposition, 152
  and value statements, 163, 164
Standard Bank, 104
Start-ups, 4
Starwood Hotels, 104
State Farm, 172
"State of Email Marketing By Industry, The"
  (Pay), 43
Stone, Oliver, xvi
Strategic Account Management Association
  (SAMA), 248
Strategic questions, 146–147
Stumpf, John, 72
Success, patterns of, 88
Sun Yat-Sen, 103
Sunseeker, 104
Sunset Project, 23
Supercell, 104
Superdrug, 104
Supplier drivers, 68–69
Supply Chain Management, 2, 69
Supply Chain Reengineering, 68
Sydney, 22
Symantec, 17
Syngenta AG, 104

T

Taiwan, 10, 103
Telecom, 90
Television advertising, 5
Tencent, 104
Texas, 92
Thailand, 10
Three-step marketing model, 34–36, 35f
Tianjin Tianhai Investment Development Co., 104
Time magazine, 93, 105
Tommee Tippee, 104
Total Quality Management, 2, 68
Toyota/Lexus, 172
Track records, 87–88
Trusted Advisor(s)
    adding value as, 185
    and Client Value Zone, 127
    credibility of, 123
    and demonstrating integrity/capability in subsequent meetings, 195
    described, 20–23
    examples of, 155, 186
    and going back over old ground, 164
    objective of becoming, 126
    and personal relationships, 129, 187
    and research, 55, 74
    sense of purpose in, 113
Tumblr, xvii
Twitter, 183, xvii

U

United Kingdom, 64, 103
University of North Carolina (UNC), 6–8, xii
University Sales Center Alliance (USCA), 249
U.S. Bureau of Labor Statistics, xviii
USA Today, 30

V

Value
    being able to deliver, 121, 122
    citing past, 113
    communicating, to executive, 195–196
    company resources as source of, 155–156
    company solutions as source of, 156–158
    and credibility, 123
    demonstrating your, 114
    elements of, 154f
    framing your, 131
    and loyalty, 172
    perception of, 148
    personal, 154, 155

    selling, 150
Value creation, 38–40, 88, 144–167
    hypothesis for, 150–151
    with new ideas, 185
    proposition for, 151–162
    statement for, 163–167
    and structuring meetings with executive, 145–150
Value hypothesis, 150–151, 165
Value Nexus, 157f
Value proposition, 151–162
    and connecting needs with capabilities, 153
    customer-focused, 159f, 161f, 162
    differentiation of, 154–156
    sample, 160f
    specific measurements in, 151–152
Value Proposition Worksheet, 221
Value statements, 163–167
Vax, 104
Vimeo, 57
Vine, xvii
Volvo, 104
Vorsight, 31

W

Waldorf Astoria, 104
Wales, 64
Wall Street, 91
Wall Street (film), xvi
Wang Deyuan, 105
WebEx, 183
Websites, 31–32
Weetabix, 104
Welch, Jack, 18
Wells Fargo, 72–73
Who Says Elephants Can't Dance: Inside IBM's Historic Turnaround (Gerstner), 85
Wiko, 104
Will, exertion of, 90–91
Working backward, 58–59
World Scientific Publishing Company, 89
World Trade Organization, 92, 103, 136
World Triathlon Corp, 104

Y

Yahoo, 73
Yahoo Finance, 179
YouTube, 5, 57, xvii

Z

ZDNet, 182
Zhu Di, 102

About the Authors

Nicholas A. C. Read is chairman of the sales training firm SalesLabs and former executive director of Ernst & Young's global revenue growth advisory practice. His early career was in international B2B sales and management in the advertising, communications, financial services, and software industries. A visiting professor at the Russian Presidential Academy of National Economy & Public Administration in Moscow and an executive MBA lecturer at Kingston University in London, his strategic thinking and research on sales transformation and technology-enabled sales coaching has been a subject of interviews and presentations on television, radio, magazines, and conferences that include *Forbes*, *In Washington Tonight*, *The World Financial Review*, and the British Academy of Management. He is a cocreator of the award-winning ROCKET sales skills coaching platform, plus training workshops that include *Professionalism in Sales Management* (PriSM), *Target Opportunity Selling* (TOS), *Selling to the C-Suite* (S2C), and *The Architect Leader* (TAL) delivered to professionals in more than 40 countries. Learn more at www.saleslabs.com.

Stephen J. Bistritz, EdD, spent more than 27 years with IBM in numerous senior roles in sales training, direct sales, and sales management. He later served as vice president of development at OnTarget Inc., for the bestselling *Target Account Selling* (TAS) and *Selling to Senior Executives* (SSE) workshops, which have been delivered to tens of thousands of professional salespeople worldwide. Steve has authored articles for publications such as *Marketing Management Magazine,* the *Sales & Marketing Executive Report*, the *Journal of Selling & Major Account Management,* and SAMA's *Velocity* magazine. He has spoken at conferences for numerous organizations including Microsoft, Abbott Diagnostics, IBM, SAMA, and ASTD. He holds a doctorate in human resource development from Vanderbilt University and lives in Atlanta with his wife, Claire, three grown children, and six grandchildren. He is currently president of his own sales training and consulting firm based in Atlanta, Georgia. Learn more at www.sellxl.com.